PRESENTED TO

_____

FROM

_____

DATE

_____

Books by

Wayne Holmes

FROM BETHANY HOUSE PUBLISHERS

The Heart of a Father
The Heart of a Mother
The Heart of a Teacher
The Embrace of a Father

WAYNE HOLMES has served as a children's and youth pastor. His writing has appeared in periodicals and *Ripples of Joy,* a story collection. He directed the Greater Cincinnati Christian Writers' Fellowship for five years and is currently involved with Toastmasters. Wayne, his wife, Linda, and their family live in Cincinnati, Ohio.

The EMBRACE *of a* FATHER

TRUE STORIES
of Inspiration & Encouragement

COMPILED BY
WAYNE HOLMES

BETHANYHOUSE
MINNEAPOLIS, MINNESOTA

Published by Bethany House Publishers
11400 Hampshire Avenue South
Bloomington, Minnesota 55438

Bethany House Publishers is a division of
Baker Publishing Group, Grand Rapids, Michigan.

Printed in the United States of America

ISBN-13:   978-0-7642-0056-4
ISBN-10:   0-7642-0056-9

DEDICATION

Dedicated to my dad,
Denver Holmes, Jr.,
and to my father-in-law,
Charles E. Miller

$\mathcal{A}$CKNOWLEDGMENTS

Special thanks go to my mom and dad, Joyce and Denver Holmes, who took me to church and introduced me to their God.

I also want to say thanks to my father-in-law, Charles (Chuck) Miller. You've become a good friend.

To my writing friends and mentors I owe a large debt of thanks: Cecil (Cec) Murphey, Bob Hostetler, Michael Brewer, Joe Lacey, and Dan Edelen.

To Julie Smith, Kyle Duncan, and the team at Bethany House, thank you for partnering with me on another project. As always, you've been a delight to work with.

Karen Solem and her assistant have faithfully guided and supported my writing career, and I am indebted to you.

My family has patiently allowed me to pursue my writing, and I am grateful for your sacrifice and understanding.

Finally, I want to express deepest appreciation to my wife, Linda. You have been God's richest blessing upon my life.

CONTENTS

SECTION TEN: TRUSTING A FATHER

SECTION ELEVEN: THE EXAMPLE OF A FATHER

SECTION TWELVE: THE EMBRACE OF A FATHER

$\mathscr{I}$NTRODUCTION

I haven't always been the perfect father. In fact, I've never been a perfect father. I tried, but too often I failed.

The task of gathering stories from the lives of earthly fathers that reflect the image of the heavenly Father intimidates me. If I failed in being the perfect father—and I did—and if my own father failed to be the perfect father—and he did—then is it possible for anyone to set the proper example of fatherhood so that we may get a glimpse into the heart of our father God?

That is the challenge I faced. No earthly father is perfect. But there are times when a man rises above the ordinary and does something so wonderful that we are awed by his act of selfless love. "If God is like that," we think, "then I want to know him, *be* like him, love him, and be loved by him."

I love stories. I love to read stories, hear stories, and share stories. Some of the most significant changes in my life have been accomplished because of a story. My hope is that through this collection of anecdotes, the reader may come to a deeper knowledge of the heart of God. I pray that through the stories the reader will experience the embrace of the Father, and will remember that God is always ready to wrap us in his love and hold us in his care.

—*Wayne*

A FATHER'S
*L*OVE

Manhood at Its Best

J A M E S   D O B S O N

from *Stories of the Heart and Home*

How can we get a handle on the ephemeral qualities of character and strength in a man of God? It is understood most readily by observing a good *model*, and I crossed paths momentarily with one of the finest a few years ago.

My family had joined me at Mammoth, California, for a weekend ski outing. The kids were still young, and I was working frantically to teach them the fundamentals of the sport. That's a tough assignment, as every skiing father knows. You can guess who gets to carry all the skis, boots, and poles, and then park the car, stand in line to buy the lift tickets, herd the clan toward the ski slopes, and get everyone zipped up and ready to go. At that precise moment, inevitably, one of the children announces that he or she has to go to the bathroom. Upon hearing that important news, Dad clomps back down the hill with his child in tow and then goes through the zippety-zip process twice more. Then he trudges back up the mountain. That is how the system works on a good day.

On a bad morning, some of the most frustrating experiences in living can occur. Children are fully capable of announcing this need to visit the "john" one at a time, sending Dad up and down the mountain like a yo-yo. By the time he and the last child get back, the first one has to go again. Kids seem to delight in losing valuable equipment, too, such as leather gloves, designer wool hats, ski jackets, etc. They're also good at bickering, which drives their harried parents crazy.

On the particular day in question, it was a bad morning for my family. Our children did everything wrong. There we were on a family vacation to produce a little togetherness, but I couldn't stand either one of my kids. They complained and dawdled and spread clothes all over the city of Mammoth. Maybe it will make other families feel better to know that the Dobsons have nerve-wracking days like that. By the time I transported the family to the ski lodge, I was well on my way to total irritation. Danae and Ryan climbed out of the car with a grumble, and I headed toward a parking lot a mile or so away. On the way down the hill, I muttered a brief prayer. Actually, it was more an expression of exasperation than anything else.

"What am I going to do with these kids You've given to me?" I said to the Lord, as though it were His fault. He did not reply.

I parked the car and walked back to an assembly area where a flatbed truck comes by every ten minutes to pick up passengers. About fifteen skiers stood awaiting a ride up the mountain, and I quietly joined them. Then I noticed a "different" young lady standing with the others. She turned to look at me, and I observed the unmistakable appearance of mental retardation in her eyes. This late teenager was behaving in a very strange way. She stood facing the mountain, quoting the word whomever over and over. "Whomever!"

she said in a loud voice. A few seconds later, she repeated the word nonsensically.

Having worked with developmentally disabled individuals for years, I felt an instant empathy for this girl. It was apparent, however, that the other skiers didn't share my concern. They were young, attractive, and beautifully outfitted. I watched them glance in the direction of the girl and then take a step or two backward. They rolled their eyes at each other as if to say, "Who's the 'crazy' we have with us?"

About that time the truck arrived, and all of us began climbing onto its bed. As the driver took us toward the ski lodge, the retarded girl continued to face the mountain and say the word whomever. By this time she stood alone, as the "in crowd" left her isolated at the center of the bed. She was alone, that is, except for a big man who stood nearby. Suddenly, I realized that he was her father.

It was at that point that this man with the kind face did something I will never forget. He walked over to his daughter and wrapped his arms around her. He put his big hand on the back of her head and gently pressed it to his chest. Then he looked down at her lovingly and said, "Yeah, babe. Whomever."

I must admit that I had to turn my head to conceal the moisture in my eyes. You see, that father had seen the same rejection from the beautiful people that I had observed. He saw their smiles . . . their scorn. His act of love to the girl was only partially done for her benefit. The father was actually speaking to all of us.

He was saying, "Yes, it's true. My daughter is retarded. We can't hide that fact. She is very limited in ability. She won't sing the songs. She won't write the books. In fact, she's already out of school. We've done the best we could for her. But I want you all to know something. This young lady is my girl, and I love her. She's the whole world to me. And I'm not ashamed to be identified with her. 'Yeah, babe. Whomever!' "

The selfless love and tenderness of that father flooded out from his soul and engulfed mine. Instantly, I felt compassion and love for our two children.

"All right, Lord!" I said. "I get the message."

Two weeks later, I was a guest on a national television show, and the moderator gave me four and a half minutes to answer such questions as "How did the institution of the family get into such a mess, and how can we correct the problem?"

I couldn't have answered the question in four and a half hours . . . but I can say this: One of the solutions to family disintegration has something to do with what that father was feeling for his handicapped girl, there in the back of that flatbed truck. That kind of unconditional love will heal a troubled home. It will resolve conflicts between parent and child. It will even help us cope with a tragedy like mental retardation.

PARENTAL MATH

BOB BENSON

from *See You at the House*

Nearly a week ago Peg and I had a very hard week.

Wednesday night—Mike slept downstairs in his room where children belong and we slept upstairs in ours where moms and dads belong.

Thursday night—We were 350 miles away and he was in Ramada 325 and we were in 323 in connecting rooms and we left the door open and talked and laughed together.

Friday night—700 miles from home and he was in 247 and we were in 239 but it was just down the balcony and somehow we seemed together.

Saturday night—He was in the freshman dorm and we were still in 239.

Sunday night—We were home and he was 700 miles away in Chapman 309.

Now we have been through this before. Robert had gone away to college and we had gathered ourselves together until we had gotten over it—mainly because he is married now and he only lives ten miles away and comes to visit often. So we thought we knew how to handle separation pretty well, but we came away so lonely and blue.

Oh, our hearts are filled with pride at a fine young man and our minds are filled with memories from tricycles to commencements, but deep down inside somewhere we just ached with loneliness and pain.

Somebody said you still have three at home. Three fine kids and there is still plenty of noise—plenty of ball games to go to—plenty of responsibilities—plenty of laughter—plenty of everything *except Mike*. And in parental math five minus one just doesn't equal plenty.

And I was thinking about God. He sure has plenty of children—plenty of artists—plenty of singers—and carpenters—and candlestick makers—and preachers—plenty of everybody *except you*. And all of them together can never take your place. And there will always be an empty spot in his heart and a vacant chair at his table when you're not home.

And if once in awhile it seems as if he's crowding you a bit—try to forgive him. It may be one of those nights when he misses you so much he can hardly stand it.

"JUST LOVE HER"

BARBARA M. HALLER

With clenched fists she stomped through the toddler years. Our daughter Katie was a courageous climber: up the stairs and out of a crib before she could walk, scrambling onto tables and kitchen counters.

With a steel will, our determined daughter had no intention of conforming to the expectations of anyone, especially me. She insisted on wearing her socks inside out, and with arms crossed she sternly told me at the shoe store that I'd "be wasting money buying those shoes because I'm *not* going to wear them."

Katie scribbled precious, primitive notes to me, threatening to run away from a life made miserable by three bothersome big brothers. "But I know you'd miss me" was her tender postscript.

Some nights as I lay in bed, a sense of defeat enveloped me. I knew God should have the victory in this battle with Katie's will. But I stubbornly thought that God fully trusted *me* to do the job. I cried to my husband, Bill, "She baffles me; what should I do with her? Does she need more discipline, or less? Do I need to lighten up?"

"Just love her" was his three-word cure. How his quick-fix annoyed me! To me, "just love her" was on a par with permissiveness.

In my mind, Bill had the easier end of the loving deal. The revelry started after dinner each evening as four kids romped with Dad in the family room. Diving off sofas and rolling in pillow piles, our children squealed with wild abandon as Bill led the charge through hours of fun.

On the weekends I gladly turned Katie over to Bill. Ashamedly, I derived some secret satisfaction when my husband's calm demeanor was ruffled by our daughter's emotional tidal waves. *Now* he knew what *I* was up against all week. Though tense with frustration, somehow he could muster up his motto and "just love her." Her tears soon turned to giggles and I was left baffled.

One Saturday night Bill's love-cure was severely tested. As he filled our large tub with bubbles and bath toys, three-year-old Katie took her battle position. "Wash my hair? Make me!" she seemed to say.

"Katie, your hair needs to be washed," Bill told her firmly. He coaxed and teased to no avail. She would not be swayed by his usual tender tactics.

Soon the scene escalated into one of thrashing arms, flying bubbles, dripping walls, and one drenched daddy. Katie's shrieks reverberated throughout the house. I hoped the neighbors couldn't hear the commotion.

Determined to subdue her and accomplish the task, Bill stripped off most of his clothing and climbed into the tub with our hysterical daughter.

From my spot in the hall I soon heard not one, but two people crying. Katie's howls mingled with the long, deep sobs of my husband. As I peered around the corner, I gasped to see the two of them, a sopping, sobbing mass of intertwined bodies. At last, our little girl surrendered and leaned into her daddy, relieved to be controlled and comforted by his strength. I sighed with gratitude that I'd married a man with an amazing capacity to put aside his frustration and intensely love our willful daughter.

The moment reminded me that God never gives up on us. He weeps over our disobedience and waits to enfold us in his loving arms. He accepts us even when we are obstinate, screaming, and thoroughly unlovable. God wants us to realize our utter helplessness and lean fully on his strength. Through our messiness and moping, our tirades and tantrums, he loves us. He just loves us.

Katie is now in high school, and her tantrums are a distant memory. God used my daughter's willfulness to build in her the strength of character she needs to resist negative peer influences. We still have a few battles of the will, but in the end we both realize that God has the final say.

The love that Bill poured into Katie must have filled her to the brim. It spills out as she calls from her room at bedtime, "G'night, Mom and Dad. I love you!"

The eternal God is your refuge, and underneath are the everlasting arms.
(Deuteronomy 33:27)

THE UNSEEN FATHER

PHILIP YANCEY

from *Disappointment With God*

One holiday I was visiting my mother, who lives seven hundred miles away. We reminisced about times long past, as mothers and sons tend to do. Inevitably, the large box of old photos came down from the closet shelf, spilling out a jumbled pile of thin rectangles that mark my progression through childhood and adolescence: the cowboy-and-Indian getups, the Peter Cottontail suit in the first grade play, my childhood pets, endless piano recitals, the graduations from grade school and high school and finally college.

Among those photos I found one of an infant, with my name written on the back. The portrait itself was not unusual. I looked like any baby: fat-cheeked, half-bald, with a wild, unfocused look to my eyes. But the photo was crumpled and mangled, as if one of those childhood pets had got hold of it. I asked my mother why she had hung onto such an abused photo when she had so many other undamaged ones.

There is something you should know about my family: when I

was ten months old, my father contracted spinal lumbar polio. He died three months later, just after my first birthday. My father was totally paralyzed at age twenty-four, his muscles so weakened that he had to live inside a large steel cylinder that did his breathing for him. He had few visitors—people had as much hysteria about polio in 1950 as they do about AIDS today. The one visitor who came faithfully, my mother, would sit in a certain place so that he could see her in a mirror bolted to the side of the iron lung.

My mother explained to me that she had kept the photo as a memento, because during my father's illness it had been fastened to his iron lung. He had asked for pictures of her and of his two sons, and my mother had had to jam the pictures in between some metal knobs. Thus, the crumpled condition of my baby photo.

I rarely saw my father after he entered the hospital, since children were not allowed in polio wards. Besides, I was so young that, even if I had been allowed in, I would not now retain those memories.

When my mother told me the story of the crumpled photo, I had a strange and powerful reaction. It seemed odd to imagine someone caring about me whom, in a sense, I had never met. During the last months of his life, my father had spent his waking hours staring at those three images of his family, my family. There was nothing else in his field of view. What did he do all day? Did he pray for us? Yes, surely. Did he love us? Yes. But how can a paralyzed person express his love, especially when his own children are banned from the room?

I have often thought of that crumpled photo, for it is one of the few links connecting me to the stranger who was my father, a stranger who died a decade younger than I am now. Someone I have no memory of, no sensory knowledge of, spent all day every day thinking of me, devoting himself to me, loving me—as well as he could. Perhaps, in some mysterious way, he is doing so now in another dimension. Perhaps I will have time, much time, to renew a relationship that was cruelly ended just as it had begun.

I mention this story because the emotions I felt when my mother showed me the crumpled photo were the very same emotions I felt that February night in a college dorm room when I first believed in a God of love. *Someone is there*, I realized. Someone is watching life as it unfolds on this planet. More, Someone is there who loves me. It was a startling feeling of wild hope, a feeling so new and overwhelming that it seemed fully worth risking my life on.

A FATHER'S
*W*ISDOM

THE BOAT WILL FLOAT

PENELOPE J. STOKES

— from *Beside a Quiet Stream* —

In recent months not one but two television networks have produced movies about Noah and his enormous boat.

It's not exactly the *Titanic*. No one falls overboard and drowns. The boat doesn't sink in a grand display of special effects. It's simply a story of audacious obedience to God, who knows what the future holds.

Noah, the Bible tells us, was a righteous person in an unrighteous world. When the Lord gave him the command, he gathered materials and built the ark to specification, rounded up the animals and his family, and waited. And then it happened. "The fountains of the great deep burst forth, and the windows of the heavens were opened. The rain fell on the earth forty days and forty nights" (Gen. 7:11–12 NRSV).

Noah had faith. He had no outward sign the flood was coming—not so much as a cloud in the sky. He didn't really understand what the future would bring, but he responded to God. He built the ark, and then entrusted his life and the lives of those he loved to the boat. He didn't steer, didn't create maps and charts for the journey, didn't try to figure out where they were going. He just watched while God shut the door and waited as the ark was born up on the waters and set down again on the mountain.

My dad taught me a similar lesson when I fished with him as a young girl. "Trust the boat," he told me. "If something happens and we capsize, the boat will float. Hang onto it—don't strike out on your own."

Our lives, even as Christians, are fraught with uncertainty. Storm clouds gather. The rains begin to fall. Lightning and thunder strike fear into our hearts and make us tremble at the looming possibilities. God doesn't reveal the future to us, doesn't tell us what is going to happen or how things will turn out. But the Lord does give us assurance that when the floods come, we will be born up and brought to a new place in our relationship with God.

Resist the temptation to strike out on your own. Have faith. Wait.

Sooner than you expect, the waters will subside.

THE FATHER AS JUDGE

BRYAN DAVIS

from *The Image of a Father*

A s fathers we are household judges. Although we have no formal training, no plaques on the wall reminding everyone of our advanced degrees from the great university of fatherhood, we dutifully climb into the judge's chair. Without a gavel, without a bailiff, we have the responsibility to hold court. Wearing a long, black robe might help. It could create an air of authority, but I think it would draw more giggles than respect. Yet, even without a visible symbol of our judicial mandate, we're called to divide between truth and error, to render impartial verdicts and deliver just punishments or rewards.

In Perry Mason's court battles, the judge had it easy. The brilliant attorney always managed to extract a confession from an unsuspecting witness, and his client invariably walked away a free man. With a pound of his gavel, the judge just said, "Case dismissed," and the newly revealed criminal was led to perdition, his head bowed and his hands cuffed.

I, on the other hand, have found that our in-house court dramas sometimes end with a roll of the dice rather than a strike of the gavel. I simply have no idea what to do. Black and white melt into gray as my children pour out an avalanche of explanations that justify their behavior, at least in their own eyes, and sometimes in mine if their stories make sense. When stories conflict, not only do I have to be the judge, I have to be both advocate and prosecutor, sometimes for more than one child at the same time.

At times like these I have to remind myself that being a judge is a fatherly calling, a role of my heavenly Father that I reflect. God is certainly One who expects us to give an account for our actions, and I model His judicial position for the sake of my children. Of course, I'm not the Supreme Judge. Since I can't know the hearts and minds of my children perfectly, I have neither the ability nor the desire to take that role. I'm more of a surrogate judge, disciplining with fairness and consistency to the best of my ability. As a surrogate judge, I receive my authority from on high and exercise it in humility, understanding my imperfect perception, but not shirking my responsibility even if I have to mediate disputes I would rather avoid.

For example, on an innocuous level, there's the ever-present "Who gets the toy?" feud. Upon hearing a cry from across the house, "He's mine! I had him first!" I know it's time to adjudicate another case, this one being submitted to the court docket as "The Case of Mr. Bunn, a stuffed rabbit." When I walk into the room, the child who's actually holding Mr. Bunn displays eyes of innocence, her smile proving that even a four-year-old understands the maxim "Possession is nine-tenths of the law." Her accuser, red-faced and pointing a shaking finger, lays out the case for the prosecution. "She took Mr. Bunn from me. I had him first."

Ah, the "I had him first claim." I've heard this before. Priority claim on a stuffed bunny is a powerful start for the prosecution's case.

The defendant shakes her head and closes her eyes. "It doesn't matter. I got him for my birthday, so he's mine."

The ownership defense in its purest form.

"But it was sitting on the floor all morning. She can't expect to be able to grab it anytime someone picks it up."

Score one for the prosecution. Casting aspersions on the owner's integrity.

The debate can go on and on, and a father might be tempted to grab Mr. Bunn around his velveteen belly, making his blue button eyes bug out, and yell something like, "If you two can't get along, Mr. Bunn is going to do a belly flop from the roof of the Empire State Building!"

Would I ever actually say that? Well, maybe not. But I'll bet real judges are tempted to say far more than "Order in the court!" Our real response may require the wisdom of Solomon. What would he have done? I suppose offering to cut Mr. Bunn into two equal pieces might work, but our savvy kids have probably already heard about Solomon's strategy, and the attempt could backfire, as follows.

"I'll tell you what," I say, placing Mr. Bunn in a sitting position on the table. "I'll cut him in half and give each of you an equal share."

Their eyes light up. In unison they shout, "Cool!" And one child runs away calling, "I'll get the hacksaw," while the other flattens Mr. Bunn on the table, his arms and legs spread out to await his untimely demise.

Such is the life of Judge Dad, the guy who now has to buy a new Mr. Bunn.

Seriously, this scenario is not far from reality. Difficult decisions face us on a daily basis, some having more eternal consequences than deciding Mr. Bunn's fate. And what if we make a bad decision? Will our children suffer because of our mistakes? Possibly, yes. But as we trust our Supreme Judge to correct our surrogate errors, we move on to the next case. Our fallibility is no excuse for avoiding our responsibility. Abdication of the judge's chair is not an option.

TAKE THE WHINING OUT OF WORK

JEAN LUSH

with Pamela Vredevelt

from *Mothers & Sons: Raising Boys to Be Men*

I grew up in a beautiful subtropical town where my dad was the head of an agricultural school. He was wonderful with boys and taught the young men to love work. He managed his four children the same way he did his schoolboys, and also taught us to enjoy hard work.

I vividly remember an incident that happened one Saturday morning during my childhood. The day was blazing hot. Most folks determined to accomplish their tasks before midday. As we were finishing breakfast, Daddy peered out the kitchen window and said, "Whew! It's going to be another beast of a day. The weather is much too hot for children to go out in the garden. I'll go out and hoe the vegetables alone. This job must be done today." Then, with a gleam in his eye, he said, "Children aren't tough enough for this job. You stay in the cool house; I'll do it alone!"

In protest we said, "We're tough, Daddy! We aren't sissies in the heat!"

"No, no, children," he argued. "I cannot let you help me today." Glancing out the window again, he lowered his voice. "What a shame. I hate hoeing alone on Saturdays!"

"But Daddy, we want to go with you!" we exclaimed. With a hint of surrender in his voice, he warned, "It's a sunburn kind of a day." We pleaded and assured him that we liked suntans. A funny smirk crossed his face, and he finally gave in to our begging. "Well, perhaps you can join me in the garden, but all of you must put your sun hats on first."

Father was not dumb. He knew exactly how we would respond, having done this many times before. Now, follow me into the garden.

It was blistering hot, and all of us perspired heavily. Daddy gave us each a long, wide row to hoe, and he hoed the middle row in between us. A minute didn't pass without him coaching us: "You children are great. I want to let you in on a secret: I never worked like you when I was your age. I dodged these jobs and left your two uncles to do it all. I liked to slip away and shoot rabbits instead!" (Grandmother Hilton said he stretched the truth. He really worked very hard as a child.)

"Do we really work better than you did, Daddy?" we asked.

His encouragement continued: "You children are great little workers. My goodness, my hoe bumped something, but I can't find it. Would someone come over here and look around where I've been working?"

Hunting around a thick tangle of peas on pruned branches, my brother Murray suddenly blurted out, "Wow! I found a big cold bottle of lemonade! How did this get here? Dad, Dad, can we have this?"

"Goodness me," Daddy replied, "I have no idea how this got here. But I brought the garden mugs, so why don't we all sit down near the big fig tree and take a rest?"

After our thirst was quenched, we finished raking the vegetable patch while Father commented on the way we handled our hoes, taking time to teach each of us. We never knew we were being taught, because Dad made learning a happy experience. We probably did a lousy job completing work assignments now and then, but he never said we performed poorly. He always found something good to commend and showed us how to make improvements.

With a full morning of work behind us, we followed Daddy into the house. As he walked through the front door, his words echoed through every room. "Edith, where are you? I have a fine band of workers here, and we're all hungry. These children are great helpers. I could never have managed on my own." By now we were red-faced and wilted, but we felt like Australian pioneers, proud of our accomplishments.

ADDICTED TO ACHIEVING

KEVIN LEMAN

from *What a Difference a Daddy Makes*

When Holly first went away to college, our firstborn, straight-A student started pulling all C's. Years later, she was asked about this—specifically, how I reacted. This is how she responded:

"My dad didn't overreact. His attitude was more, 'They're your grades and it's your life; if these grades aren't good enough, you'll either bear the consequences or get the awards.'"

Throughout their schooling, I imprinted my daughters with the value of a good education. But I never led them to believe that grades were all that mattered. In fact, I sometimes went overboard in the other direction. When our kids got their report cards, they knew I paid more attention to the teacher's written character comments than I did to the actual grades. I wanted our children to know that what matters is the type of person you are, not the things you do.

We live in a society, however, that usually focuses on how much we can get done, and our children pay the price for our polluted perspective. A typical afternoon cell phone conversation goes like this:

"Bob, where are you?"

"I'm at the gym. Where's Ashley?"

"No! Monday night is karate! You're supposed to be at the rec center. Her teacher just called."

"I thought Monday nights were basketball."

"That's Tuesday, after Girl Scouts. You better get over to the rec center fast!"

"All right, I'm headed back to the car. By the way, what are we having for dinner?"

"I don't know. Megan's band practice is running late. Why don't you stop and get some burgers?"

If you tie a kid's self-esteem to achievement, you'll run the little buzzards ragged trying to find something they can excel in. That's why the Lemans aren't joiners. If you really want to help your kids, let them choose one extracurricular activity a semester.

The curse of suburbia is forcing kids to succeed outside the family. With country folk, there's a much more healthy emphasis on giving back to the family. A child's sense of worth and belonging comes from contributing to the home life in which she has been nurtured and cared for. Her contribution might be as simple as milking a cow, feeding the chickens, or collecting eggs, but such a child grows up with a sense of belonging and purpose.

What can you do in the suburbs? Take out the garbage? Great— what will the kids do for the remaining twenty-three hours and fifty-five minutes of the day?

Somewhere around the 1960s, suburban parents found the "answer": Kids need to prove their worth outside the home. We have to find something they're the "best" in. If they fail at basketball, baseball, gymnastics, track, soccer, and chess, we try Girl Scouts, drama, piano lessons, art, spelling bees, you name it. And, whether we want it to or not, all this frenetic activity says one thing to our kids: Prove yourself.

I'm so glad I serve a God who says, "Kevin, I've proven my love for you," rather than "Prove yourself, Leman."

If you want to raise a well-adjusted daughter, don't run her into exhaustion in a vain effort at helping her finally prove herself. Prove your love. Prove your commitment. Prove your affection. That's what builds healthy kids.

THE

$\mathcal{D}$ ISCIPLINE

OF A FATHER

DADDY'S LINE

JEAN MATTHEW HALL

Our house was small and modest. We had no grassy lawn; our yard was black dirt. A huge ancient oak tree sheltered our front yard and deprived the ground beneath it of sunshine and grass. But the oak gave us shade from the heat of the scorching Florida sun and shelter from the daily showers. It gave my sisters and me a wonderful place to play, and I loved that tree.

We didn't have a fence around our yard either; that was a luxury we couldn't afford in 1954. But we lived on one of the few paved roads in Hart Haven, Florida, and my Daddy was very conscientious about protecting us from the traffic on that road. He couldn't protect us with a fence of wood or stone, so he protected us with his presence and watchful eyes.

Many summer evenings my little sisters and I played under the oak tree; we chased each other around squealing and laughing. Mama stayed inside the house doing dishes, and Daddy stood outside with us as we played. He drew a line in the black dirt with his shoe and told us it was the fence. We were never to cross that line without a grown-up holding our hand. Even if the dirt drifted and covered the line, we were to remember it was there and never step over it. Then Daddy planted himself between the line and the road, and watched us play for an hour or so until the sky melted from powder blue, to dusty pink, to indigo.

Occasionally I got caught up in play and forgot about the line. I might run over it or just step on it. Somehow, Daddy always knew when I did, and he took that opportunity to teach me about boundaries. He didn't yell at me or spank me. He simply left his position of standing guard, walked over to me, took me by one arm, and bent down to look me straight in the eyes. "Where's the line, little girl?" he asked sternly. "What could happen if you forget and run out into that street when a car is coming?"

I looked into those steel-blue eyes and mumbled something like, "I could get killed."

Then his eyebrows arched up and his lips closed and squeezed tight against each other like the jaws of the cast iron vice in his workshop. Without saying another word, he reminded me of all the warnings and all the dangers out in that big, black road. Then he pulled me close, gave me a hug, and shooed me off to play again.

No humiliation or punishment, just a consistently administered reminder *every* time I forgot. I remember more than once chasing one of my little sisters around the tree and coming dangerously close to Daddy's line. But I also remember screeching to a halt and stopping just short of the line, then looking around to see Daddy standing nearby, arms crossed, eyebrows up. Watching. Protecting. Teaching. Loving.

A shy smile would crease my lips, then I would make an about-face and run away from the road—laughing and squealing with delight again, safe under Daddy's watchful eyes and consistent discipline.

As I grew older the lines drawn in the dirt changed, but Daddy never did. He drew the lines, then he enforced them with consistency, firmness, and love. He kept me safe from many potential dangers in this big, black world. And I thank God for it.

In my mind I can see Daddy standing in front of that road in his smutty work clothes, arms crossed over his chest, watching our every move as we played. Standing tall behind him I can see the shadow of my other Daddy, my heavenly Father. Watching. Protecting. Teaching. Loving. Drawing the lines and keeping me safe from this big, black world for all of my fifty-six years.

$\mathcal{I}$S THERE SOMETHING YOU SHOULD SAY TO GOD?

B R U C E   W I L K I N S O N

from *Secrets of the Vine*

I magine a sunny day in Indiana. Darren, twenty-five, has driven up from Memphis to see his dad, whom he's hardly spoken to for years. They're out in the driveway shooting a few hoops. Finally Darren gets out what he has driven so far to say:

"Dad, I didn't understand you for years. I didn't know why you had so many rules for me in high school—about parties, TV, chores, driving, money. I didn't like your expectations. I thought you were mean and stupid. I said terrible things about you behind your back. And, Dad, I'll admit that I hated you at times. But now I see that you were just trying to be a good dad. You only wanted what was best for me. You never gave up or gave in.

"I came here to apologize for what I have thought and said about you. I was wrong. I know I hurt you very deeply, and I'm sorry."

I believe that the majority of believers need just such a conversation with their Father. I remember the day I finally made amends with God over how I had been treating Him. That was many years ago, and I can tell you that it has radically improved my relationship with God.

Isn't it amazing that God allows Himself to be hurt by us? (We know this happens because Ephesians 4:30 says, "Do not grieve the Holy Spirit.") It's hard to comprehend God's tender love in the face of our misunderstanding, repeated rejection, and unwarranted abuse from us. Yet His love remains constant!

If your relationship with your Father is injured, I encourage you to apologize today for your attitudes and thoughts. Tell God you have misunderstood His actions and badly misjudged His character. Tell Him exactly how you have felt and why, and ask Him for His forgiveness.

$\mathcal{P}$ICTURE PERFECT

JEAN DAVIS

I took my camera to church Sunday morning to try to capture a repeat of the most amazing worship I had ever seen. At the previous Friday night's session of a women's conference, the two-year-old grandson of one of the participants grabbed a tambourine and shook the instrument in time with the music. Later he picked up a three-foot banner from the front of the church and waved it as we sang.

On Saturday night, when the music started, the same boy flourished a green banner. Then another toddler went forward, grabbed a banner the color of his orange pacifier, and joined in worship. When the second boy's four-year-old brother joined them, I stared in amazement. Three young children stood in front of the sanctuary making bold, sweeping movements with brightly colored banners while we sang.

On Sunday morning, when the music began, the three boys stepped forward, one by one, to pick up banners for worship. *What a perfect example of unity in the Spirit,* I thought. As I took my camera from its case and held the viewfinder to my eye, I noticed a boy about five years old joined them.

As soon as the four boys got together, their mission shifted. The newest member straddled the staff of his banner. The worship team now had a new leader, and they followed him.

Four colorful banners on dowels became stick horses with flowing manes, and could those horses go! The ride must have been exhilarating. Even from where I sat, I could see the eyes of the youngest boy sparkle as he threw back his head and laughed.

As these mighty men of God galloped across the front of the church, the predictable happened—one horse bumped into another. Whether the insult was accidental or not, a minor skirmish began. First one boy and then the others took their strong steeds in hand and transformed the dowels into dueling swords.

Three or four good whacks landed before the father of the oldest boy made his way to the front. The man's reaction surprised me. I thought he might bend over to the child's level and, with red face and gritted teeth, reprimand him. I thought the dad might take the child back to his seat by way of the bathroom for an attitude adjustment. I thought he might send the other boys back to their parents.

None of that happened. Instead, the father simply removed the banner from his son, took him by the hand, and walked him to a row of empty seats on the side of the platform. The boy, quite subdued, sat on the floor at his dad's feet. As the worship service continued, the dad stood with the rest of the congregation and waved the banner over the child.

Though I didn't get the photo I had hoped for, I did get a clear image of God. How grateful I am that his banner over us is love, even when we are being disciplined.

THE FATHER AS SAVIOR

BRYAN DAVIS

from *The Image of a Father*

E very now and then I get a feeling that something is bothering one of my children. Whether it comes from knowing them so well or from a nudge from God's loving Spirit, I can't always be sure. On one occasion in particular there seemed to be a shadow in my son's countenance, a shift in his mood, a subtle turn in his expression that made me take notice. I felt God's Spirit telling me to check it out, because this latest turn wasn't an insignificant shift. Something was clearly wrong.

I asked him what was on his mind, inviting him to sit with me for a couple of minutes. He made an effort to gently shrug off my inquiry, giving an anatomical smile and an excuse for his altered demeanor, one he may have believed himself. He was not convincing. As I gazed into his eyes, I felt the Spirit of God come upon me, telling me exactly what was troubling my son. Somehow I was able to identify the darkness that painted his shadows. I questioned him about the subject directly, speaking with love and compassion, yet with a depth of power that made me tremble inside.

Being confronted directly with his sin struck him to the core. He turned red and began visibly shaking. He cried, nodding his head in confession, his face contorting in pain. As he confessed his sin, pure anguish poured forth, and in his agony he cried, "Please hit me!"

Oh, the grief that stabbed my soul! Clearly, this poor child had suffered for so long, and I was unaware! He begged to be punished, to suffer for his sin. He believed that pain would relieve his guilt, a bruise or a bloody nose to make amends for his iniquity. Yet, I knew it would not bring true healing. It would be a mere bandage for a heart that needed God's holy surgery. Someone had already suffered for his sin, had already shed His blood so my son would not have to bleed.

I grasped his shoulders and joined him in his sorrow. "No!" I cried, tears streaming from my own eyes. "It's not punishment you need. You need forgiveness and cleansing from sin." He wept on as I begged God to give me words of wisdom. Again I felt His Spirit touch my lips. "Don't you see?" I continued. "It's not so much the rules I want you to keep. I want your heart! Rules are good, but if your heart doesn't belong to God, rules make you a slave. God wants your heart first! God wants a son, not a slave."

The cooling refreshment of God's holy breath passed through the room, bringing its healing touch. I believe my son reached a turning point that night. Although I had taught these truths many times, he finally experienced the truth firsthand, feeling God's piercing sword and then His healing balm.

There is no doubt that my son experienced the depths of his own darkness, the painful squeeze of Satan's cruel cords of bondage. He felt judgment, the weight of the law condemning his soul, and he begged for release. In the torment of his imprisonment, he reached out for the only remedy that made sense, a buffeting blow of punishment, something, anything, that would give him the beating he knew he deserved. Maybe then the unreachable standard could be appeased. Maybe then he could find release from his chains.

But such a beating isn't what God demands for the contrite. The gospel of Jesus Christ doesn't scourge with a whip or clap a new lock on the chains of a slave; it freely offers redemption and the inheritance due a son. The prodigal son begged to be taken in as a lowly slave, but his father gave him a ring and a fatted calf, welcoming him home with open arms.

Our heavenly Father doesn't rejoice in punishment. He longs to distribute gifts of love, as Jesus said,

> Or what man is there among you, when his son shall ask him for a loaf, will give him a stone? Or if he shall ask for a fish, he will not give him a snake, will he? If you then, being evil, know how to give good gifts to your children, how much more shall your Father who is in heaven give what is good to those who ask Him! (Matt. 7:9–11 NASB)

It seems that when we ask God for a stone of judgment, He offers us the bread of life. Such is the nature of our loving Father in heaven. Such is our nature as earthly fathers if we imitate His providing hand of grace. Yes, we should be prepared to punish disobedience, but even more important, we must be ready to offer forgiveness, reflecting God's role as Savior to our repentant children.

LESSONS FROM A FATHER

JUST WAIT TILL JANUARY

KAY SHOSTAK

———◆———

Your Mama and I want you to wait a little while to get your ears pierced."

I rolled my eyes. "How long? My birthday is in two weeks."

Daddy flicked the turn signal, looked back over his left shoulder, and eased into the other lane of the highway. He passed the slower car and pulled our brown '68 Ford station wagon back into the right-hand lane before answering. "Just wait till January."

"January? But that's forever!" Daddy had picked this isolated time as he drove me to church youth group to answer my plea for pierced ears. I slumped back against the seat and crossed my arms.

Looking out my window at the hills of brown grass, dry from the August heat, I shook my head. *January's too far away. I have to change his mind.* I concentrated for a moment on swallowing the tears I usually depended on. Daddy didn't fall for emotions. He needed calm reason and facts. Luckily, I'd prepared my argument well.

I took a deep breath and turned to Daddy. "If I get them pierced for my birthday, I can ask my friends to get me earrings for presents.

Then when Christmas comes I'll get the other stuff I want, like an earring holder." Economics usually worked with my dad. In my house we only received gifts for birthdays and Christmas. I closed my mouth and looked straight ahead. I'd never played poker, but I knew when to be quiet.

Hot wind from the open window ruffled the short sleeves of Daddy's checked shirt. "Tell you what," he finally said. "You wait until January and I'll pay to get your ears pierced and buy the earrings and other stuff you would've gotten as gifts."

In my mind I had already moved on to my next argument, but his offer jerked me back. If I wait until January, I could get gifts for my birthday and Christmas *and* pierced ears *and* earrings *and* an earring holder? Daddy must be slipping. I started to ask him to repeat himself, but I didn't want him having any time for second thoughts. So I shut my gaping mouth and shrugged. "Okay, I guess I can wait."

When we arrived at the church, I leaped out of the car. My friends were going to be so jealous. My ears were as good as pierced! As Daddy pulled away, I watched the car for a minute and sighed. Poor Daddy—so ignorant of the way the world worked.

School started at the end of the month, and it seemed like every day another friend showed up with her ears pierced. Tonya, one of my best friends, had beautiful blue eyes. For her September birthday she got blue birthstone earrings. Of course they were set in silver, to match her braces—junior-high fashion heaven! Every time I saw her, I dreamed of my January windfall.

However, one day in October Tonya came to school sporting a white bandage on one ear instead of the delicate blue earring. Infected? No one ever said anything about pierced ears getting infected.

Ellen, in my biology class, turned out to be allergic to cheap metal. Back then, only expensive earrings were hypo-allergenic—

expensive, old-lady earrings. No cute little ladybugs or dangling rainbows for Ellen.

January 1975 came and went. I didn't mention earrings. Neither did Daddy.

Four more Januarys passed and earrings once again looked like a good idea to me. I wanted to get my ears pierced, but what was Daddy going to say? Hesitantly, one night after supper, I entered the living room and approached him with my request.

"Sure," he said, without even looking up from his newspaper.

"What? Did you say 'sure'?" I walked over to the couch to sit down. "This was such a big deal last time. What's so different?"

Daddy laid down his paper and leaned forward in his easy chair. "I never was against pierced ears. I just didn't think you knew enough to make that decision back then. Waiting until January gave you a new perspective, didn't it?"

"Wait." I shook my head. "How did you know I would change my mind?"

Daddy shrugged. "I didn't. If you'd still wanted your ears pierced in January I'd have kept my end of the bargain."

He grinned as he leaned back in his chair and lifted his newspaper. "Always remember, it's amazing how things can change if you just wait a little while."

I wandered back to my bedroom and lay down on the bed. Somehow my talk with Daddy made me feel grown up. Daddy believed I was more mature than that twelve-year-old that wanted pierced ears. He acted like I was perfectly normal. *Really though,* I sighed, *how much did he know about teenage girls?* I started to sit up, then stopped as I remembered that car ride four years earlier. Sitting in the front seat of our car I absolutely knew what I wanted, but Daddy knew what I needed—a little time. I sat up as a grin stretched wide. Okay, so Daddy might know a little bit about teenage girls.

I've heard that God answers prayers in one of three ways: Yes, No, or Wait. Like my daddy, God knows saying "Wait" isn't just to show me who's in control. Sometimes, he knows I'm just not ready to hear "Yes."

GOD'S CREATURES GREAT AND SMALL

HELEN KAY POLASKI

O ne bright summer afternoon my younger sister and I raced
through the back door of our cinder-block house, letting the
screen door bang loudly behind us. In the way of children, Pam and
I were oblivious to anything except our next adventure, and the lure
of the lush green outdoors was too great to ignore. Our bare feet
scarcely touched the warm grass as we embraced the wind—heavy
with the scent of growing things—and hastened to reach the
meadow that butted against our yard.

The moment we stepped into the meadow we flung ourselves
facedown on the path that ran through the center and immediately
burrowed into the tall grasses and wild flowers that grew as tall as
our shoulders. Pretending we were baby bunnies, we crawled on our
elbows toward the heart of the meadow. We stopped frequently to
rest and to watch honeybees and bumblebees as they extracted pollen
from the various flowers that bobbed on slender stalks above us.

Dazzled by the great outdoors and intent on our play that afternoon, we weren't looking for a lesson or expecting to save anyone or anything. But in the way of the world, a lesson was panning out before us, even as we played. As is natural for a couple of five- and six-year-old children, we were curious about every creature that entered our world. It didn't matter if the creature was another human being, a stray cat or dog, a wild animal, or even an insect. We had been taught from an early age that our time on this earth was to be spent doing good deeds and helping one another. We believed that philosophy. While we played we kept an eye out for all of God's creatures.

Lying in the tall grass, our faces pressed against the warm sand, we became one with the meadow. Our breathing matched the sigh of the wind as it swept over us. We whispered encouragement to the ants as they worked, our hearts beating in time to the chirp of the crickets and the buzz of the grasshoppers. Of all the insects in the meadow, it was the bumblebees that captured my attention. They were round and fluffy, and the drone of their wings mesmerized me.

If I could have been anything other than a child, I would have wanted to be a bumblebee.

Moments later, we were surprised to hear the familiar roar of our father's truck as he drove past the meadow and pulled into our driveway. From the position of the sun, we knew Dad was home earlier than usual. Most mornings he left before the sun rose and didn't get back until the sun was well below the horizon. Rising from our hiding place, we scurried toward the path that would lead us home. As soon as we stepped onto the path, I saw the bumblebee lying on the hard-packed ground. The bee's black gossamer wings were silent, its chubby body curled into a ball.

I squatted to get a closer look. Pam stopped, too. After a moment, she bent down and blew on the bee gently. The insect's legs worked feebly, but it didn't get up and fly away. Pam and I exchanged a look.

"It's hurt," I said, tears springing to my eyes.

I couldn't leave the bee on the path; someone might step on it. The right thing to do was to help. As carefully as I could, I picked up the bee and cradled it in the palm of my hand.

Dad would know what to do.

I had taken only a few steps when a stinging sensation in my hand caused me to cry out in pain. To my horror, the bee had stung me and was now stuck fast in the soft flesh of my palm. Screaming in pain, I shook my hand. The bee dislodged—leaving a black stinger behind—and flew away. With tears flowing down my cheeks, I ran to the safety of my father's arms.

I found Dad sitting on the front porch. Seeing my tears, he immediately lifted me onto his lap.

"What happened?" he asked as I held my hand up and showed him the bee sting. Gently but swiftly, he extracted the stinger. "You got stung?"

I nodded.

"There was a bumblebee on the path so she picked it up," Pam explained while Dad bent down and dug up a small amount of dirt.

He cupped the dirt in his hand and then spat into it to make mud. A soft smile tugged at the corners of his mouth as he smeared the soothing mixture over the bee sting. "What did you think would happen if you picked up a bumblebee?"

My eyes grew large. "I was helping it," I said. "It shouldn't have stung me!" Pam crawled up onto his other knee, her eyes solemn. I could tell by her expression that she didn't think the bee should have stung me, either.

"You scared him," Dad said. "He didn't know you were trying to help him."

A new burst of tears flowed down my face. "But I was helping him. You're supposed to help everyone," I protested.

Dad chuckled and hugged me to quiet my tears. "Yes, you want to help, but you can't hold a bumblebee in your bare hands. It didn't know if you were going to hurt it or help it. You have to be careful when you help someone—especially when that someone is a bumblebee."

As his words settled inside my head, I sniffled. I had meant to help the bee and had only succeeded in frightening it. Dad tickled me to divert my attention, and I pressed my face into the warmth of his shoulder.

"Next time there's a bumblebee in the path, are you going to pick it up with your bare hands?"

I wiped my face, looked up into my father's blue-gray eyes, and shook my head. "I'll use a stick!"

He chuckled again and looked at my sister. She flashed him a grin and soon we were all laughing. Pam and I were happy to know we had done the right thing in helping the bumblebee, and Dad was pleased because he knew that the lesson he was trying to teach us had sunk in.

Just as our heavenly Father is careful when rescuing his children from dangerous situations, we also must be careful when helping our fellowman, or beast, or insect. I have continued to help bumblebees and all manner of creatures that have found their way onto my path. Sometimes I still get stung, but in my estimation it has always been worth it to know that in some small way I have been able to use God's teachings to help another.

THE PRICELESS VALUE OF AFFIRMATION

GARY SMALLEY & JOHN TRENT

from *Leaving the Light On*

*E*ven *the smallest act of affirmation can bring large benefits to a child.* How tiny those seeds can be! A woman we know had a very poor self-image as a junior higher. Because of several childhood illnesses, she was pale, thin, and underdeveloped for her age. An alert pastor's wife, however, found something to compliment. Stopping the girl in church one Sunday, the woman said, "Teri, you look so good with that red hair band. I think red really compliments you!"

The comment only took a few seconds and is now decades in the past. The junior high girl is now a wife and mother. Yet if you would look in her closet, you would immediately see a predominance of red. She has felt good about herself wearing that color ever since.

Opportunities to affirm are varied, but it takes an awake, perceptive parent to maximize the moment. Kids look to their parents to put the events of their lives—the ups and downs—in context. Mom or Dad have the opportunity to *frame* and give meaning to such occurrences. It takes a loving, attentive parent to take a common stone and make it into *a milestone* in a son or daughter's life.

This might be particularly true in the teenage years. At the tender age of sixteen, everything in life seems somehow magnified. The smallest setback or put-down can be devastating. The most insignificant slip or failure can be terminally embarrassing. At the same time, the least bit of encouragement—from the right person at the right moment—can become hugely significant.

Boys and girls in their mid teens are standing on a tightrope between childhood and adulthood—and something always seems to be shaking one end of the rope or the other.

A few years ago, I (Gary) watched my youngest son out on that shaky tightrope—and frankly wondered how he was going to do. Through his sophomore year in high school, Michael's principal desire seemed to be remaining *invisible*. His grades were so-so. He was content to stay in the background of things. He played several sports, but never seemed inclined to excel. His motto seemed to be, "Just make it through."

Then, the summer before his junior year, something amazing happened that dramatically changed that attitude right in front of our eyes. At Kannakuk Camp in Branson, Missouri (what we feel is the top Christian sports camp in the country), Michael was elected "Chief" of his high school camp, after being one of five nominees in a group numbering over three hundred.

Before the announcement, he was beside himself with excitement at his nomination, yet he always added in every conversation, "Yeah, I know I won't win."

Yet win he did—the first time he had ever won anything in his life. He was stunned! It was unquestionably one of the greatest days of his life. But when I think about it now, how easy it would have been for Norma and me, vacationing in a cabin near the camp, to have minimized or overlooked that moment in our son's life. I might have said . . .

"Huh? Oh yeah, that's great, Mike. Boy, did you see that eagle flying over the lake this morning? Did you see the size of that thing? It must have been . . ."

"Chief? Hey, way-to-go. Norm, did you want to go into Branson and do some shopping this afternoon?"

"Well, let's not get too carried away, Michael. This is just camp, remember? Now if you'd just apply yourself a little harder in school you might . . ."

Michael looked to us to *interpret* that honor by his peers. To put a frame around that day in his life. Was it a big deal, or wasn't it? Did it really say something about his potential, or didn't it? We could have easily—and inadvertently—destroyed that moment by preoccupation with other things. Instead of turning on a light in his life, we could have put that light out, perhaps for the rest of his life.

But after missing too many other opportunities to affirm my kids, I was determined not to miss this one. I almost came unglued, I got so excited about it. We all hugged him, congratulating him endlessly. One of our dear friends, Jim Shaughnessy, pitched in and said, "Great, Mike! Nothing that big has ever happened to me!"

The very next day I went to a local wood artist and had him carve a large plaque with an Indian head on it. I bought some paints and painted the feathers of the headdress, and then inscribed the plaque with a message:

CHIEF SMALLEY
Kannakuk Camp
Summer 1988

To this day that plaque hangs in a prominent place in Michael's bedroom.

But something happened that summer that was more significant than a memento on a wall. The change in my son's life was staggering. You could almost see him say to himself, *Maybe I am capable. Maybe I can accomplish some things.*

He went on to become student body president of his high school, played on a championship varsity basketball and football team, was elected homecoming king, and got serious about his grades and about preparing for the university. This domino reaction all started with that first "little" domino at camp ... an ordinary stone along the path that became a milestone.

EVERYWHERE ALWAYS

SHARON M. KNUDSON

What was that terrible noise? It was 4:30 A.M., and it woke me from a deep sleep that only a teenager can experience.

Forcing myself out of bed, I stumbled down the stairs. A constant, ear-splitting racket came from my parents' bedroom. I opened their door and was temporarily blinded by the high-wattage bed lamp clipped to the top of the headboard.

The noise was deafening. Their clock radio was blaring full blast. Old-fashioned fire alarm bells attached to the back of the headboard were clang-clang-clanging. The vacuum cleaner stationed beside their bed was not moving, not cleaning—just wailing. The cacophony of sounds terrified me. Meanwhile, the coffeepot perked madly in the kitchen, sending a pungent aroma throughout the house. Dad's timer devices had done their job to get everything going at once.

But my parents just lay there—mouths gaping open, eyes closed, bodies disheveled and limp.

Surely they could hear all that noise.

Or were they dead?

I stood still for a moment—scared and unable to move. Then I rushed over and shook my dad's shoulder.

"Daddy, Mama, wake up!" I cried. "Don't you hear all the noise?"

My parents roused themselves quickly.

"What's wrong?" Mother said. "What's the matter?"

Then it hit them: It was time to get up and milk the cows.

"Go to bed now," Dad sighed, "and thanks for waking us up."

I remember feeling guilty as I trudged up the stairs. Mother and Dad had to get up and do chores while I slept in and then went to high school. I'd always known they had an alarm system to rouse them from exhausted sleep, but I'd never seen so many noisy devices rigged together at once, nor heard them clamoring for so long.

In many ways our farm was more than a man, his wife, and five children could handle. Large by Wisconsin standards in the 1950s, we had 350 acres, and our thirty-five cows had to be milked twice a day. We grew all our own crops—enough hay, oats, and corn to feed all the livestock, which included our dairy herd, the chickens, and pigs.

From childhood on we were ingrained with the nonstop cycle of seasons and tasks inherent to farm life. Each day, immediately after school, we'd change into barn clothes and go outside for chores. Everyone in the family was expected to help.

Dad was skinny, almost gaunt, and his hands trembled from continual stress. He never rested except to sit down for a quick meal. All day long, his hurry-up strides carried him from one task to the next. There was always a piece of machinery to repair or an animal to doctor. When he wasn't within sight of the house, we knew he was back in the fields—plowing, planting, harvesting, or mending a fence.

Mother worked right alongside Dad. She was in the barn for

every milking, and she drove a tractor in the fields. In addition, she kept a clean house and took care of us kids. She made all the meals and baked bread, cakes, cookies, and bars. She also tended, harvested, and preserved fruits and vegetables from our half-acre garden.

No wonder Mother and Dad were so tired.

Toiling alongside my parents day after day, I found it natural to talk to them about whatever was on my mind. Both were sympathetic listeners and very wise. My dad was a quiet man, serious, and introspective. He had a kind face with the hint of a smile.

Since evening chores were always a family affair, I relished those rare times when I was the only person helping Dad in the barn. He kept a smooth, even rhythm as he worked his way down the long row of cows, hoisting the heavy milking machines from one cow to the next. Years of habit made this an excellent time to talk. It also made me feel grown up and privileged, being in the presence of a sage.

"What if Russia invades the United States and takes everyone captive?" I asked.

"Who will ever want to marry me?" I'd wonder a few minutes later. "I'm not pretty like the popular girls. What if I end up an old maid?"

I had other concerns too. I was well aware of the financial pressures my family faced.

"What happens if we can't pay off the farm?" I'd ask. "How can I possibly go to college with four younger kids coming behind me?"

None of my grave concerns upset my dad. He would listen intently and think for a while. Then his eyebrows would twitch and he'd say something profound. Each time, I'd hang onto his words, quickly memorizing them to ponder later.

After a while, after I'd examined my teenage turmoil for too long and he'd given me all the answers he could, he'd say in his kind, simple way, "Try not to worry so much. Everything will turn out just fine. You'll see."

I wondered how he could know that, but I sensed it was time to move on to other, more cheerful topics. After all, Daddy's world was far more complicated than mine.

Dad seemed to know everything, and I encouraged him to give lengthy answers to my questions. He had firsthand knowledge of so much. As he shared his views, my perceptions of him and the world took root. I came to understand that in his endless hard work, he was taking care of his family and building a future for us all. I saw into the heart of the man.

But the best part of my conversations with Dad in the barn was how he made me feel—like I was an integral part of things. Just by working beside him I felt mature, important, and essential to his life.

Many years have passed since my days on the farm. Now I can look back and see that everything did turn out all right. I'm a wife and a grandmother, I went through college and have been gainfully employed, and the Russians never invaded the U.S.

Clearly, those early images of my dad and the farming life cultivated in me a clear understanding of my heavenly Father. Scripture tells me that God is hardworking and diligent, patient and wise. He's involved in his children's lives and provides them with what they need. He even advises and comforts when life's questions seem too hard. He is everywhere always—but unlike my parents, he never gets tired.

I've also learned this: If ever I will stop plowing through my day and make time to be alone with Jesus, that familiar connection infuses me with peace. How gratifying to realize that as I listen and obey, he calls me, confides in me, and includes me in his plans. To him, I'm important, I'm essential.

I am loved.

A FATHER'S FORGIVENESS

THE WAY HOME

MARTHA ROGERS

G ood morning, Baby," my dad greeted me when I walked into the kitchen. He turned from the stove with a plate of scrambled eggs and set them on the table.

I grimaced and sat down. I was almost twenty years old, and Dad still called me "Baby." I didn't mind it as much as I pretended. After all, he was up at five in the morning so I could have breakfast before leaving for my nursing classes at the medical center.

That was one of the times my dad lavished his love on me. Although my parents divorced when I was ten years old, my dad and I remained close. Even after he remarried, I knew I could depend on him for love and support any time I needed it. He taught me to drive a car and to manage my finances. He taught me about God and made sure I attended church, both as a child and a teenager.

Dad supported my decision to change my major and drop my nursing classes. He helped me find a job in the summers so I could continue my studies. After I graduated from college, I moved to Houston, Texas, to begin my career as a home economist.

Dad carried my possessions into the new apartment and helped me settle in. On Sunday evening he prepared to drive back to Dallas, and gave me a big hug. "Remember to call me whenever you need anything. I'll be there for you."

I figured I was now an independent young woman and wouldn't need him anymore. The problem was, I did the same with my heavenly Father. I figured I could make it on my own as a young adult out to conquer the world.

Not many months passed before I found myself deeper into alcohol and partying than I could ever have imagined. I had moved to Houston in June, and by October I had still not joined a church in the area. I had too much fun on Saturday nights, and there was no one to force me from bed and to church on Sunday.

The further I drifted from God, the further I drifted away from Dad too. Even though I had always been a "Daddy's girl," I no longer needed to depend on him. Or so I thought.

When I became depressed and unhappy in October, I recognized the loneliness I was feeling being away from my family. So I called Dad and told him I planned to come home for a few days because I was not well.

His words cheered and comforted me. "I'll be at the airport to pick you up. I love you and can't wait to see you."

During the trip home I felt this huge emptiness inside, but didn't know what I wanted or needed. What could fill that void of loneliness?

At the arrival gate, there stood my dad. A big grin split his face when he saw me. He stretched out his arms. "Welcome home, Baby."

I didn't realize how much I had missed hearing those words. He wrapped his arm around my shoulders, and we headed for the car. In the parking lot he stopped and stared at me. "Martha Baby, I don't know what's troubling you, and you don't have to tell me. Tell

God about it. I'll be praying for you while you're here. I love you, and God loves you. Let him help you, and I'll be here if you need me."

Dad knew I was hurting, but he didn't try to find out why and give me all kinds of advice. He said what I needed to hear: "Tell God all about it."

That weekend turned into a pivotal time in my life. Knowing my dad loved me and prayed for me gave me the incentive to seek forgiveness from my heavenly Father. Dad did not condemn me and neither did my Father. Unconditional love was a gift from both my earthly and my heavenly Father.

Dad did not mention my problem for the remainder of my visit, but before we left for the airport I told him what had happened in my life in Houston. I asked him to forgive me for disappointing him, just as I had asked God to forgive me for sinning.

"I love you," he said. "You'll never disappoint me as long as you remember whose you are and what he did for you."

When I walked toward the gate to board my plane, Dad hugged me. "Baby, I can see it in your eyes—God answered my prayers and yours. I see peace there, and I'll be praying for you every day."

"Oh, Dad, I love you, and thank you for being so understanding and not nagging me all weekend. The problem is not completely gone, but God will help me get rid of it."

"That's what I wanted to hear. Now go on back to Houston and show them what you can do." He kissed my forehead, and I headed for the plane.

On the plane the words to a song I had learned in college filled my mind. I knew God had a plan for every creation and knew the course of every river's journey. He had a plan for me and knew my journey; how could I not follow him?

I took care of the last remaining bit of my problem as soon as I arrived back in Houston. I hailed a cab and asked the driver to take me to the church near my apartment for their Sunday night service. I joined the church that night and gave my life anew to God's service. Dad's love sent me back to my Savior and heavenly Father, where I found a peace that has never left me.

Dad has since gone on to be with Jesus, but his love and his prayers will be a part of me until the day I die. Just as Dad's love will not leave me, neither will my Savior's love. Thank you, Dad, for showing me the way home.

MIRROR, MIRROR

JILL BAUGHAN

I've always been a lazy little goof-off at heart. When I was six years old, it got me into trouble.

I loved sweets, especially Dum-Dum suckers. I used to sneak them out of the candy dish in the kitchen and off into the living room, where I ate them as I watched TV. Knowing that I would get into trouble for my contraband food, I had to be creative in hiding the evidence—the sticks and wrappers. This required a little trial and error in my mind. Should I stuff them in between books on the bookshelf? No good. You could see that the books weren't closing all the way. Should I shove them under the couch? That would be okay as long as my mother never ran a vacuum cleaner there. She was very clean, however.

Finally, I came upon a brilliant plan. My parents' bedroom was right off the living room, and the door was conveniently located close to the TV. On the back of the door hung a full-length mirror—the perfect place to hide the evidence! I was jubilant because I figured that I could probably hide wrappers and sticks behind that mirror till I graduated from high school, and no one would be the wiser.

Of course my mother discovered them one day, told my father, and he called my brother and me into the living room for a confrontation. Since my brother, Ted, was six years older than I, knew everything, and was innocent of the crime, I decided that I'd follow his lead in responding to Daddy's interrogation.

"All right, who did this?" he asked, looking us over for incriminating facial expressions.

"I didn't do it, honest," said Ted.

"I didn't do it, honest," said I, doing my best to look wide-eyed and innocent.

I could tell he was surprised that neither of us was willing to confess, and I wondered what on earth he could do about it. Punish us both? Or take a guess and punish the more-likely liar, since he had a fifty-fifty chance of convicting the real criminal? The last thing I expected him to do was what he did.

Nothing.

After a minute of looking back and forth at us, he simply said, "Okay," and he let us go.

I couldn't believe it! I was off the hook! Guilty, but not charged! Life was good.

For a while. About five minutes, maybe. Then I started to feel as guilty as I was. All day I avoided Daddy at all costs. Around two in the afternoon, I was playing (okay, *hiding*) in my bedroom when he appeared in the doorway. He only wanted to ask me something entirely unrelated to The Deed, but as soon as I saw him, my "guilt reflex" kicked in. In a panic, I threw my hands up in the air like I'd been caught robbing a bank, and shouted, "I didn't do it, honest!"

I think this is what tipped him off.

Still, he said nothing to me about the matter; he only wanted to know how I was doing.

I lasted about three more hours—three more hours of beating a hasty retreat out of whatever room he entered, three more hours of explaining to Barbie and Ken why I was forced to tell an untruth to my father, three more hours of imagining the spanking to end all spankings that would surely be mine if I owned up. Finally, around five o'clock in the afternoon, I could stand the tension no more. I would confess, I decided, because anything was better than this distance I had put between Daddy and me, not to mention the tension that was destroying every effort I was making to have a Saturday of quality play. Nervously I tiptoed into the kitchen, where he was sitting at the table with my mom.

But before I could say a word, he motioned for me to come to him. Bracing myself as I made my approach, I thought, "This is it. I've been had. I might as well gear up for the spanking of my life." To my surprise, though, instead of turning me over his knee, he picked me up, set me in his lap, and whispered in my ear, "Why don't you tell Mommy it was you who put those sucker sticks behind the mirror?"

At that invitation my heart burst, and I cried tears of relief, confessing that I was the one who did it and deserved to go to jail. Fortunately, he didn't think jail was warranted; he just let me sit on his lap till I calmed down. Then he took my hand, led me into the bedroom, and said, "Why don't we clean up this mess together?"

Even though it was considerable work (I *had* done a magnificent job of sticking and stuffing), I didn't mind. My relationship with my father was right again, and that's what mattered most to me.

Four years later, when I was only ten, he died suddenly, but that simple act of grace lives on as one of my most treasured memories. I have replayed that day many times in my heart as a practically perfect picture of forgiveness.

And I love thinking that God, too, invites me—whether I've

bumbled up at six or sixteen or sixty—to come to him, and even sit in his lap, as he whispers in my ear, "Why don't you just own up to that colossal misjudgment you made? You'll have to clean up the mess, but I'm here with you; I forgive you."

And with that forgiveness comes freedom—the freedom to forgive myself, to move on, to know real joy, and to make sure there's plenty of quality playtime for the lazy little goof-off who still lives inside me.

THE WAY THAT HE LOVES

NANCY HAGERMAN

———◆———

Daddy was a big man. He loved fancy clothes and flashy cars. The eleventh son of an itinerate preacher, he grew up in poverty and learned to work hard for what he wanted. As a young man he was personable and charming, an excellent salesman.

Rheumatoid arthritis struck him in his early twenties. He tried to continue working, but the pain became too intense. He was in the hospital when I was born.

He slept during the day because the pain kept him awake at night. It hurt him when I sat on his lap. Hospitalizations were frequent, and Daddy became depressed.

"Don't bother Daddy, honey. He needs to rest," Mom told me often. I grew up not knowing him well and being a little afraid of him.

That's why I was surprised when I faced up to my stupid mistake, and why my first car accident provided a lesson in God's grace.

I was sixteen and sitting proudly behind the wheel of my father's brand-new Cadillac convertible. Its white top was spotless, and the metallic turquoise finish sparkled in the sun with tiny flecks of silver. With my new driver's license tucked safely in my purse, I was elated about driving Mom to the store for the first time.

Mom securely belted into the passenger seat, I drove to the end of the block. Stopping, I looked carefully before turning right. As we rounded the corner, my door flew open. Reaching with my left hand to close it, I continued to turn.

The car jumped the sidewalk and ran through a chain link fence. Metal screeched against metal as the fence lifted and tore across the hood, making deep scratches like giant fingernails. I could hear the fabric rip as the fence slashed its way through the canvas top, then continued on, raking gashes across the trunk.

Paralyzed with fear, I stared straight ahead as the car continued to move forward. Only inches from our neighbor's dining room window, my mother, using her most commanding voice, said, "Nancy LoRayne—stop this car!"

The police came, filled out their report, and we returned home. Mom sent me to talk to my father—alone.

Trembling, I approached our front door as though I were taking my final walk on death row. He would be waiting on the other side, and I was guilty without excuse. The accident didn't even involve another car. It was totally my fault.

Crying, I opened the door. Dad looked up from the newspaper and asked what was wrong. Through tears and sniffles, I blurted out, "I had a wreck."

Dad was on his feet in an instant, walking toward me. I winced, expecting punishment. Instead, I was in his arms. He wanted to know if I was all right. He never asked about the car or even seemed to care. I was safe and that's what mattered.

It's like that with God. He constantly surprises us with his love. Through mistakes, trials, and heartaches, we can draw near to him and rest in his arms. Not because we are good, but because he is our Father.

DADDY'S BABY GIRL

DR. DEBRA PEPPERS

I was born on Father's Day, Sunday, June 18, 1950. Until I reached my terrible teens, I had always been "Daddy's baby girl!" I wish now I could go back and relive those rebellious years, for I would never have chosen to be a high school dropout and runaway—especially back in the late '60s in my small hometown of Clarksville, Missouri. In that idyllic *Leave It to Beaver* town, population 500, nobody did such things.

I saw myself as the family outcast, since my older sister, Donna, was valedictorian, head cheerleader, prom queen, and a size eight. My younger brother, Duke, was athletic, good-looking, and the sports superstar of the town. And then there was "poor Debbie," as I was often called. At 250 pounds, drinking and running away became a way of life—my way of escape.

Like the proverbial prodigal, I eventually returned home, where my parents welcomed me once more. With their help, I was reinstated in school and paradoxically went on to complete not only high school but also receive three college degrees.

Now that I am a retired high school teacher, having dealt with many students of today with similar problems to mine, I realize there was not much help available when I was a teen. Neither my parents nor I had positive coping skills back then. They tried everything they knew to do, but nothing seemed to help.

The following letter was written by my precious, loving daddy when I was a senior in high school, but I didn't get it until twenty years later. My mother told me she had been saving it for "just the right time."

My Darling Baby Girl,

I write this as you have threatened to run away again. I am leaving this on your pillow with the hope that you will get it before you leave. I know at seventeen you are a young woman now and we can't stop you from going. Your mom and I have asked ourselves a thousand times where we went wrong . . . where we failed you. I would give anything if we could go back to the days when you were Daddy's little girl and would snuggle up on my lap and bring all your hurts and wounds to me to "make better."

I only blame myself for all that has gone wrong and would give my very life for another chance to make it right. I didn't see soon enough how much you were hurting. Mommy and I have prayed and cried for you more than you will ever know and have asked if we were too strict or too lenient, too giving or not giving enough. All we know is that we love you and want you to talk to us. Please reconsider before you leave again and let's see if we can't work it out one more time.

Dearest Debbie Girl, we love you with no strings attached. God brought you to us, and no matter what, you will always be my precious baby girl. When you read this, no matter how late, please come talk to me.

Always,
Your Loving Daddy

I never received the letter that night because I had already run away again and didn't return for six weeks. However, as I said, my parents saved the letter for over twenty years, anticipating the right time to present it to me, which occurred the night of the Missouri State Teacher of the Year Banquet at the state capitol. I was honored as one of the top five teachers in the state. As my parents, husband, and family were there celebrating with me, we were asked how we survived those terrible teen years. It was only by the grace of God, much prayer and faith, that I finally graduated from both high school and college, became a teacher, lost 100 pounds, was happily married, and had the support of a wonderful, forgiving family.

Before my acceptance speech that night, my parents gave me a beautifully wrapped gift box. Thinking I might find a pendant or medal with the inscription "Teacher of the Year," or "Wonderful Daughter," I opened the box to find instead a yellowed, crinkled, tearstained letter written by my loving daddy twenty years before. I wept uncontrollably as I realized for the first time all that my parents had gone through and the road that we had all traveled to achieve the success we now experienced.

With mascara streaming down my face, I gave an entirely different speech from the one I had planned. I thanked God that my parents were finally able to see the fruits of their labor. All their past struggles, the sleepless nights, the times they helped me return to school and church, had finally been worth it. The real gift they gave me was the priceless gift of unconditional love and forgiveness.

Being a retired radio talk-show host and high school teacher, I get to travel around the world speaking and I share this letter with my audiences. Often my parents will accompany me, and my dad has to blink away tears, as I do, when I read his letter.

We recently returned from taking my parents to Europe for their sixtieth wedding anniversary, where we had a hard time keeping up with such active eighty-year-olds. When Dad is asked the secret of his youthfulness and vitality, he teasingly says, "If I can survive my daughter's teen years, I can do anything!"

In private, he still cuddles me next to him, and reminds me that he loved me as much back then as he does today. He says he always knew how special I would be when God gave him the best Father's Day gift he ever received over fifty years ago—his baby girl.

Even during the years of my rebellion and anger I had a wonderful earthly father who never judged me or rejected me. I didn't intimately know my heavenly Father, and I couldn't see the plans he had for my life until I came to Christ. Since then, not only do I know the embrace of my earthly father, but through his example I have also come to know the embrace of my heavenly Father.

I keep Daddy's letter in my Bible. It makes a nice addition to the love letters that God has written to me as well.

A FATHER'S PERSPECTIVE

$\mathcal{I}$ CALL YOU DAD

BOB ROSE

Henry, who's your cowboy friend?" I asked.

"This is Justin, Kathy's son," the proud grandpa replied as he lifted the little cowboy to sit on the parts counter.

Justin reminded me of the caricatures in "Cow Pokes," Ace Reid's cartoons on cowboy life. A beat-up felt hat shaded the biggest, bluest eyes I'd ever seen. Soft blond curls cascaded from under the band and covered the collar of his western-cut shirt. Blue jeans and boots completed the outfit. He walked with a swagger, a perfect mimic of his grandpa.

I had no idea when we met that day that in less than a year I would call that little cowboy my son. But that's what happened. I began dating his mother in the late spring. Justin made sure every outing was properly chaperoned. We went everywhere together.

We got along wonderfully, until Kathy and I decided to marry. Then, with just a few words pledged before family and friends, I became "Dad" to a two-year-old. We made it official as soon as legally allowable. I adopted Justin six months after Kathy and I married.

For all of his life Justin had his mother all to himself. They always shared a bedroom and did everything together. Though Grandma and Grandpa had cared for him on occasion, the rearing responsibilities fell squarely on her shoulders. For the most part Justin behaved well, but he didn't take to the notion of some new guy telling him what he could and couldn't do. And I felt compelled to order him around a lot. I had the crazy notion that a child could be perfect in every way if he just had sufficient parental input. The first year had many rocky times.

Justin put down deep roots. He liked his home, and he liked his friends. Once established in a place, he wanted to stay there forever. However, circumstances in my pursuit of a career caused us to relocate numerous times. With each move Justin pulled a bit farther away from me. Since my job changes brought about the moves, I held the responsibility for his discontent.

I tried my best to be a good dad, but many of my efforts failed. The summer he was eleven, no coach came forward for the Little League baseball team. Though I knew nothing about baseball, I finally agreed to step into the position rather than have the boys miss a summer of games. My ineptitude became obvious with the first game—we lost. We followed that with sixteen more defeats, most of them complete romps. While he thanked me for trying, I know Justin was embarrassed by our miserable season.

Justin's teen years brought even more trials. Justin liked solitude, and adolescence distanced him even further from me. Our conversations usually consisted of my saying something and his ignoring me. To my old-fogey ears, the few words he did utter sounded more like grunts than parts of speech.

At the beginning, Justin's birth father had no contact with him.

That changed during the spring of Justin's sixteenth year. Out of the blue, Mike called and asked if he could come over and meet Justin. Though Justin didn't seem interested in him at the time, they kept in contact.

As with many absentee parents, Mike tried to make up for lost time and attention with gifts. Each holiday, his lavish gift-giving overshadowed what our budget allowed us to provide. I didn't believe that we were depriving him (or the other boys, for that matter), but I still felt cheap in light of Mike's material outpourings.

My own deep-seated insecurities made me cringe each time Mike's name came up. I'd done my best to be a father in every sense to Justin, but I sensed a distance from him that increased with each new demonstration of Mike's generosity.

After Justin's graduation from high school, he remained in our native Wyoming to attend the University of Wyoming. Kathy, our other two sons, and I moved to Brownsville, Texas. With thirteen hundred miles separating us, and visits limited to school vacation times, we depended on the telephone to keep us connected.

During one call, the conversation seemed to center around the latest new stereo Justin had received from Mike. As the call neared an end, I said, "I'm glad that you are getting such nice things, but I hope you remember the guy who put in the time with you while you were growing up."

I heard a tiny chuckle before Justin replied, "Haven't you been paying attention? I call him Mike and I call you Dad."

Some people long to hear just three little words; not so for me. I always knew that Justin loved me. I just didn't know if he acknowledged me as his father. For me, four little words, "I call you Dad," demolished my doubts. Nothing he has ever said or done has meant more.

I can't help but wonder if God, my Father by divine adoption, would like to hear the same from me. The apostle Paul wrote, "But ye have received the Spirit of adoption, whereby we cry, Abba, Father" (Rom. 8:15 KJV). If that's our way of saying, "I call you Dad," then, "Abba, I'm really glad you're my Father."

THE CORNER CABINET

DIANE H. PITTS

I *know I can make one of those for Mama.* During a visit to his uncle's farm, fourteen-year-old Willard had seen the admiration in his mother's eyes as she commented on Uncle Tee's new corner cabinet. Willard eyed the cabinet from every angle. *She never asks for anything, especially since Dad died.* With ten mouths to feed, Velma Huff wouldn't ask for something frivolous like a corner cabinet.

Willard scrounged for a piece of charred wood from the fireplace and a slip of paper to sketch the cabinet. His keen eye figured the dimensions. Deciding he would try to build it, he quietly pocketed the design.

The next day Willard and his mother said good-bye to relatives and boarded the train for home.

"That was a lovely visit, wasn't it, Willard?" Her light blue eyes scanned the passing scenery, and she sighed. For once during the hard days of 1936, Willard saw his mother relax. He resolved even more to make something that would bring a gentle smile to her face. How he loved her and longed to ease her burdens.

Back home in Stanton, Velma Huff immediately went back to the chores and demands of a large family. Willard was up with the sun to farm the land and take care of the livestock. When plowing time came, he missed school. In the wee morning hours, or as the evening approached, Willard would take a few minutes to make the corner cabinet a reality. He used straight pins for nails and wood scraps for shelves. He finally painted the four-tiered shelf. Now it was ready. One evening he quietly carried the cabinet into the parlor. As Willard drifted off to sleep, he thought about Mama finding the cabinet.

Mama tapped lightly on the door the next morning. "Willard, wake up." He rubbed sleep from his eyes and slipped his coveralls on, careful not to wake his older brother Orbrie.

"Willard, did you make that cabinet for me?" Her eyes were soft and misty.

"Yes'um. Do you like it?"

"Do I like it? Oh, Willard . . ." Not given to much emotion, Mrs. Huff brushed a lock of hair from her son's forehead. "I love it." Abruptly she turned toward the kitchen and remarked over her shoulder, "How about getting me some eggs from the hen house, Son? It's time this household got cracking."

Willard grinned and stored her smile in his heart.

Through the years Willard continued to make things: a guitar, a toy box, a replica of his boyhood home. Each time, he took what was available and used fine craftsmanship for each project. From his perspective, he wasn't limited by what he didn't have, only by what he didn't try. His gifts extended his love to others.

As Willard's daughter, I have seen the joy he gains from being generous. In the same way, my heavenly Father must take pleasure in giving to me. The corner cabinet now rests in my home as a reminder that from God's perspective I am worth his time and affection.

SCARED GIRL TALKING

GLENN A. HASCALL

The moment I arrived home from work my daughter, Alyssa, asked: "Can I recite my poem, Daddy?"

"Absolutely not." I smiled a sly grin as I wearily shut the front door.

She utterly ignored my mock refusal and began regaling all who had ears to hear with an elaborate story of polar bears, giraffes, mice, cats, monkeys, crows, and swans—all in a well-timed, emotionally poetic voice.

"You know, Daddy, there's only two more days before the speech contest."

"Really? Only two?" I feigned surprise.

"You're going to be there, aren't you?" she requested.

"It's a busy time at work right now..." I noted her crestfallen face as I completed my thought, "but I wouldn't miss it for the world."

She giggled as she ran across the room and jumped into my embrace. Alyssa had practiced this poem for weeks, reciting it clearly and with great effect. She'd never been comfortable in front of people, but she wanted to do this. She'd recite the poem at the breakfast table as she was getting ready for school, between bites of spaghetti at supper, and before bed—almost any time there was an opening in conversation, and sometimes even when there wasn't.

The morning of the speech contest I entered the cramped classroom filled with students, teachers, judges, parents, siblings, and grandparents. Alyssa would glance at me with a special look reserved for dads and a grin for an audience of one.

After we recited the pledges to both the American and Christian flags, Mrs. Clause provided a listing of the rules. Each of the students prayed that the morning would go well and that they would all remember their lines.

The first student recited his poem while his parents made sure the video camera captured every moment. We applauded as the young man took his seat. We waited for the judges to make their ruling. The same scenario held true for students two through five. As the judges ruled on the skills of the fifth student, Alyssa's face took on a peculiar expression. She would soon walk the long row to the front of the classroom, where everyone would fix their attention on her and she would spin a memorable tale.

"Number six," came the compassionate voice of her teacher, and Alyssa began, scared girl talking.

What others saw was a terrified third grader attempting to get through her poem without hyperventilating. They heard a poem devoid of emotion. They watched a girl who didn't know what to do with her hands, and eyes that refused to focus on anything but her daddy.

The panel of judges cast quick judgment and summarily dismissed her from advancing in the competition. Observers expressed visual remorse.

What did her daddy see?

I saw a little girl tackling something uncomfortable. She had the poem memorized and didn't struggle with the words. She never asked to be excused from participating, and my heart grew two sizes in that knowledge.

But I saw more.

I saw an eight pound, seven ounce baby girl who only had eyes for her daddy. I recalled the ten-month-old girl who spoke her first word, *thermostat,* and the girl who showed me her first tooth held in her tiny hand. For a split second the contest became the embodiment of every second I had ever spent with her. In that instant I refused to notice the stumbles, the lack of inflection, the pity expressed by other parents.

I was proud of my daughter.

As she took her seat to the smattering of applause, I walked to her side. She smiled and reached out for a hug. I gazed into her blue eyes and told her how awesome she was. She beamed.

For a moment it seemed there was no one else in the room except the two of us. Perhaps in years to come, Alyssa will forget that moment. However, in the archives of my personal history, that will rank among the most satisfying. I think God the Father understood.

As a father of a little girl who faced her fears and stood up to potential humiliation, I can only imagine how proud God is of his children—of me, even when I try hard and no one else seems to notice or appreciate what I do. God knows, sees, and is proud. I want to experience the same sense of abandon that my daughter felt. I want to run to my heavenly Father, climb onto his lap, and feel the warmth of his embrace.

ONE MORE
FOR JESUS

RICK WARREN

from *The Purpose-Driven Life*

My father was a minister for over fifty years, serving mostly in small, rural churches. He was a simple preacher, but he was a man with a mission. His favorite activity was taking teams of volunteers overseas to build church buildings for small congregations. In his lifetime, Dad built over 150 churches around the world.

In 1999, my father died of cancer. In the final week of his life the disease kept him awake in a semiconscious state nearly twenty-four hours a day. As he dreamed, he'd talk out loud about what he was dreaming. Sitting by his bedside, I learned a lot about my dad by just listening to his dreams. He relived one church building project after another.

One night near the end, while my wife, my niece, and I were by his side, Dad suddenly became very active and tried to get out of bed. Of course, he was too weak, and my wife insisted he lay back down. But he persisted in trying to get out of bed, so my wife finally asked, "Jimmy, what are you trying to do?" He replied, "Got to save one more for Jesus! Got to save one more for Jesus! Got to save one more for Jesus!" He began to repeat that phrase over and over.

During the next hour, he said the phrase probably a hundred times. "Got to save one more for Jesus!" As I sat by his bed with tears flowing down my cheeks, I bowed my head to thank God for my dad's faith. At that moment Dad reached out and placed his frail hand on my head and said, as if commissioning me, "Save one more for Jesus! Save one more for Jesus!"

I intend for that to be the theme of the rest of my life. I invite you to consider it as a focus for your life, too, because nothing will make a greater difference for eternity. If you want to be used by God, you must care about what God cares about; what he cares about most is the redemption of the people he made. He wants his lost children found! Nothing matters more to God; the Cross proves that. I pray that you will always be on the lookout to reach "one more for Jesus" so that when you stand before God one day, you can say, "Mission accomplished!"

PROVISIONS OF A FATHER

SHINY SUNDAY SHOES

S U S A N   L A R E   B A U M G A R T E L

M y Sunday rush was underway. I loved my church in the city, but the thirty-minute drive stretched to forty if you hit all the lights red. The week at work—exhausting. Feeling worn and ragged, I would rather have stayed home. My commitment to leading worship in the choir kept me going.

Waiting impatiently at yet another light, my thoughts whisked back to Sundays long ago and my dad's Sunday ritual: shining our shoes in preparation for church.

The smell of shoe polish and early morning coffee greeted my brother and me as we sleepily left our rooms. *Dad's up.* The whoosh, whoosh of the buff brush and the dull clatter of Mom working in the kitchen were warm, familiar Sunday sounds.

Reid and I were silent lumps as we sat at the newspaper-draped kitchen table and watched Dad work. Experience told us breakfast wouldn't be served until the shoes were lined up in the hall. Watching Dad shine shoes fascinated me. Watching Dad do most anything requiring two hands was a study in ingenuity and determination. A farming accident the summer before his first year of college left his right arm with only a four inch stump that extended beyond his elbow.

A silent, somewhat gruff man, Dad never shared much beyond the facts. We knew when and how it happened, that he had to learn how to write all over again with his left hand, and that he refused to leave the hospital until he could tie his tie—a requirement according to the handsome young man ready to get on with life in the 1930s. Over the years he mastered great and small tasks, from carving mahogany banisters, maneuvering playing cards, and renovating houses to even removing snails from their tiny shells at an elegant dinner. Inventiveness and determination were Dad's core strengths.

Shining shoes? A piece of cake. Dad slid his stump into the toe of the shoe, holding it firmly against the tabletop. The strength and maneuverability in that arm developed through years of trial and error. His left hand dabbed and wiped the polish. Vigorous buffing brought the dull leather to a radiant, rich shine.

The blare of the horn from the car behind me jolted me back to the present. Tears dripped from my chin. Sobs rose in my throat. I missed my dad. I missed those simple Sunday mornings. I missed his arms around me. As I wept, and drove, the weight of my tumultuous week left me.

The Lord knew I needed a good cry that Sunday morning, and a sweet memory. He always knows what we need and when we need it. And he delivers at the perfect moment in time.

He stood beside my dad as he struggled with his tie. His hand was on Dad's shoulder as, hour after hour, he learned to write again. He walked with Dad as he faced his first college class and met the long stares of new classmates. From the moment of conception, the Lord planted an inventive and courageous spirit within my dad, equipping him with everything he needed to overcome a tremendous, life-altering event.

The big and the small are all important to the Lord because he loves us so.

A memory planted at just the right time.

Strength and courage to overcome defeat.

Creativity to conquer obstacles.

His provision—perfect.

Absolutely perfect.

"For I know the plans I have for you," declares the Lord, "plans to prosper you and not to harm you, plans to give you hope and a future" (Jeremiah 29:11).

$\mathcal{A}$RROWHEAD SUMMER

———————•———————

PAMELA JENKINS

I grew up in a small town on the edge of Oklahoma's Lake Keystone. It's a popular place to visit in the summer. Tourists and locals spend their days there fishing, camping, and water-skiing.

My brother and I were fortunate to be able to go to the shores of the lake all year round. We loved the names of the little coves—Appalachia Bay, Cowskin Bay, and Sandy Beach. The original community of Prue, now submerged under water, was moved to higher ground and renamed New Prue. The area was rich with tales of interesting history.

Most of the time we went to the lake when our mother was tired and needed a rest. Dad loaded us into the pickup on a Sunday afternoon, and we drove to an isolated place. My brother and I entertained ourselves by playing in the sand or running after each other around the coves. Sometimes we challenged each other to a game of skipping rocks on the water. Dad would spend the time walking slowly along the shoreline with his head bent down, occasionally kicking a loose rock, appearing deep in thought.

I still remember that summer day when I asked him, "Whatcha looking for, Dad?"

"Arrowheads." He pulled one out of his pocket and showed us a sharp stone resting in the palm of his hand.

"The Indians used these to hunt with," he explained. He let both of us hold it and test the sharpness of the point with our fingers. "When the water is low, you can find them on the shore. The water washes the dirt away and leaves them lying where you can see them."

Dad explained how the Indians would chip the flint rocks, a bit at a time, to form the arrowhead. It would then be tied on an arrow and used to hunt small game like birds and rabbits. Very tiny ones were called bird points. Sometimes the Native Americans would fashion a knife out of stone and use it to scrape hides. Arrowheads were hard to find, and spear points and scrapers were even rarer.

My brother and I decided we had to find our own arrowheads. We imitated our father's walk, kicking stones as we strolled along the shore.

We were disappointed, though. We didn't find any arrowheads that day, or the next time. Weeks went by, and we had yet to find anything that resembled a true arrowhead, although we studied rocks and tried to imagine them tied to the end of a stick and used to hunt.

One day my brother found his first arrowhead. He danced around, excited by his discovery. He showed Dad, then me, and pointed out the exact place where he found it lying on the shore near the lapping waves.

I was more determined than ever to find an arrowhead for myself. Still, they remained elusive.

One hot day we walked a long way along the beach, and then turned around to make our way back to the pickup. I was discouraged. I had spent hours looking, but hadn't found a thing.

We were almost back to our parking place when I saw something that looked promising. With my heart thumping, I bent down and touched it with my finger. I picked it up, hardly believing my luck. It was an arrowhead, all right. It was faded gray with streaks of darker rock running through it. And it was big—almost as big as my hand.

My brother's victory dance was nothing compared to the jig I performed as I showed the treasure to my family. It was the biggest arrowhead I had ever seen. What a find!

My Dad let me hold it until we got home, then he asked if he could put it away for safekeeping. He wrapped the arrowhead carefully in a piece of felt and wrote my name on it. Then he put it on a shelf in his closet.

I picked up a few more arrowheads in the years that followed, but nowhere near the amount that my father and brother found. They have beautiful framed collections hanging on their walls, a testimony to all the hours of searching the shores of that lake.

One day, as I prepared to move away to college, my father brought that old arrowhead out and asked if I remembered the time I found it.

"Of course," I told him. How could I forget that summer and my first arrowhead?

He laughed and told me the story he'd kept from me all those years. He had watched me walking, head down, along the water's edge that day. He knew I was tired and discouraged. So he cheated.

"Cheated?"

"Yes, I cheated. I walked a little ways ahead and dropped that arrowhead. I watched you walk by it twice without seeing it, but you picked it up the third time I tossed it in front of you."

I turned the arrowhead over in my hands and studied the markings on it. The edges were finely shaped and sharp enough to cut easily. There were no nicks or chips missing to mar its perfection. The size alone was enough to make it a prize. Anyone would be proud to keep it for his own collection, yet my father gave it away for the chance to see the excitement in my eyes.

Sometimes I wonder how many times my heavenly Father has placed treasures in front of my feet. Some I fail to recognize. Others I stumble over, only to realize later what a treasure was offered.

Today that arrowhead is framed and hangs on the wall of my office. Each time I look at it I am reminded of that summer day long ago and of my father's love.

THE DREAMSAVER

BERNITA CAESAR

As I rushed from my instructor's office, her harsh words burned into my soul: "You will never make a good nurse. One day you could kill somebody."

That was the Tuesday of Thanksgiving week before I left for home. At age eighteen, I'd been in my nursing program for three months, pursuing a childhood dream. I'd chosen a high-ranked school with a religious background and thought I was in the place God wanted me to be.

Thanksgiving break that year meant a special visit from a favorite aunt and uncle who were staying with us. I'd been the first one in our family to follow my dream, and the whole family was proud, especially my father.

I won't be able to face them, kept running through my mind.

"What will I tell everyone?" I asked my twin sister, Bonnie, that night as I wept in her arms. "I'm not even sure what I did wrong. My instructor gave no specific reasons for her cutting remarks."

Encouraging me to tell her everything, I related how that

particular instructor needled a group of us. While we were studying she would approach us and say, "I don't know why you're even bothering to read this; it's not going to do you any good. You will not pass."

"Please don't tell Dad," I said to Bonnie. "You know how he wants to fix everything. He will be so disappointed. When I go back next week I'll be asked to leave. The other six students aren't returning next week. They're my friends and their dreams are shattered just like mine."

Despite my plea, Bonnie told our parents. Then she told me Dad's reaction to the news. He got tears in his eyes, jumped up, and started pacing.

"I won't stand for that," Dad said. Then he hurried to his car, drove the twenty miles to the school, and went right to the director's office. Dad reported to Bonnie that the director had been surprised and speechless, now realizing why a number of other students were leaving with no clear explanation.

Dad told her how I had been detained in the instructor's office for over an hour and missed an exam. The director told my dad that no instructor was allowed to keep a student away from class for longer than fifteen minutes, and especially not during an exam.

"Tell Bernita to see me Friday after the holiday and we'll get everything straightened out," the director said.

She nodded as my father said, "I want to thank you for looking into this matter."

After looking through my records she continued, "She gets good grades and is one of the most conscientious students we have. Nursing is in her heart, and I can tell it is more than a career for her."

When Dad returned he took me aside and said, "I've been to see your nursing director and you have an appointment with her the day after the holiday." I was grateful for his intervention, but embarrassed, too, thinking he might be disappointed in me.

He said, "You've always wanted to be a nurse, and you'll be a good one. I'm sorry you've had to go through this, and I'm proud of you."

The anticipation of my meeting threatened to dampen the holiday spirit, but Dad kept the atmosphere cheerful. He acted as if he'd won a victory.

When I spoke with the director, I found she'd already terminated the instructor. Having looked into the woman's history, she discovered a background of unusual psychological behavior, which included harassment and falsified reports on a number of students.

"I know it will take time to leave the negative comments behind, but you are a good nurse," the director said. "Remember that."

I left the director's office with a renewed dream in my heart and a prayer of thanks for Dad's life-changing intervention.

For nearly forty years I have been a successful nurse, thanking and praising God for the blessing of serving him and his people in this way.

Dad has been gone for twenty years, but my heavenly Father continues to intercede for me. Romans 8:26 says, "In the same way, the Spirit helps us in our weakness. We do not know what we ought to pray for, but the Spirit himself intercedes for us with groans that words cannot express."

God is a true Father, who knows what's in my heart. He guides me and meets my needs even when I think I've disappointed him. My heavenly Father keeps me safe and secure in his loving arms, just as my dad did. He assures me I'll always have a Father to intervene, even when I think the circumstances are hopeless.

THE CHECK

KAY SPIVEY WALSH

Reaching into the mailbox, I noticed the return address of the brown envelope on top: "Internal Revenue Service, U.S. Government." Turning it over, I slid my finger under the flap. The stiff brown envelope crackled, tearing unevenly. As I pulled out my tax refund check, I smiled. Having recently finished college, the amount seemed enormous. I sobered as I remembered that, although the check was written to me, the money belonged to my dad. I owed it to him.

Four weeks ago, I walked across a stage to receive my diploma. I planned to work at a summer camp where I had been offered the position of assistant director. This job would allow me to work while continuing to search for a permanent position, but I needed a car. Considering my meager savings and lack of a permanent job, financing a car seemed impossible.

However, my dad had a way of making what seemed impossible become a reality. He offered to lend me the money to buy the car. How Dad came up with the money, I'll never know. My parents struggled to meet the college expenses of both my brother and me.

Dad and I agreed that when I received my tax refund, I would sign the check over to him as a down payment. Once I found a permanent job, I would take out a loan, pay him back, and make payments to the bank.

The day Dad and I shopped for a car was rushed because I needed to report to camp. Even so, I caught Dad admiring a yellow convertible while sending me to check window stickers for gas mileage on the more practical models. I drove away in a bright red Chevrolet sedan.

With the tax refund check in my hand, I could keep my promise to my dad. But in spite of knowing the money belonged to him, my mind skipped through the catalog pages of my wishes, wants, and even a few needs. The check was enough to support several of my dreams, including a vacation with a college friend. As for needs, the money could serve as a deposit on an apartment, but unfortunately it was not designated to fulfill dreams, but to pay a debt.

The weekend after receiving the check, I drove home in my red Chevy to visit my family. The title in the glove compartment was in my name, but in my heart I knew the car belonged to my dad. By giving him my refund check, I would come a bit closer to knowing the car was mine.

The momentary sting of giving over the money was soon forgotten in the joy of family and routine. The weekend was filled with laughter. Mom baked her famous blueberry coffee cake. As usual, I unloaded the dishwasher and fed the dog. I felt content as I packed the car to return to camp on Sunday.

When I was ready to go, my family gathered round for hugs and kisses. During this time Dad hung back, but as my mom and brothers returned to the house Dad approached. I was already in my car. Before I pulled out of the driveway I rolled down the window, wondering why he lingered.

Dad reached into his pocket and pulled out a brown envelope. It was the one with the IRS return address. He handed it to me and began to walk away. I opened my mouth to protest. Before I could voice my thoughts, he turned and answered.

"No, I don't have to do this," he said, "and, yes, I'm sure." He added, "You'll need it to make a deposit on an apartment when you start your new job."

Stunned, my hand flew to my mouth. Tears blurred my vision. As his back disappeared around the corner, I yelled, "Thank you, Dad!" I leaned back against the sun-warmed seat and whispered, "I love you too, Daddy."

Later that week I made the drive into town to run errands for camp. Taking a slight detour, I stopped at the bank.

"Deposit this in my account, please." I handed the brown envelope to the teller.

The teller returned a white deposit slip. I stared at the slip, feeling the irony. According to the rules, a check made out to me with my signature on the back belonged to me. But I knew differently. This money was only in my account because my dad had given it to me. It was only in my possession as his loving gift.

In awe, I realized this was also true of my heavenly Father. The world may see everything I have as *belonging to me*—my possessions, my job, my family. These things may even have my name on them. While I want to earn, own, and control it all, I realize that as his child, my joy comes in handing it over to him. What is truly mine comes as my heavenly Father's loving gift.

Every good and perfect gift is from above, coming down from the Father. (James 1:17)

$\mathcal{D}$AD'S SHOES

NORM WATTS
as told to C. Ellen Watts

"What are you looking for?" Mom asked as she carried breakfast dishes to the sink. She caught me rummaging through the junk drawer she had just straightened.

I stirred some more. "Mom, I need new shoes."

Locating a wide rubber band, I pulled it over the toe end of my right shoe to keep the sole from flapping. Unlike the cloth and vinyl sneakers kids wear today, school shoes in the early '40s were more like dress shoes, made of leather with stitched-on leather soles. They worked fine until you wore holes in the soles or the stitching gave out.

Mom sighed. "We bought shoes for you three months ago, Norman."

Dad slid back from the breakfast table, stood, and placed a hand on my shoulder. "Son, don't you think it's time you figured out a way to quit kicking everything in sight?"

Quit kicking? Dad had to be kidding. I'd as soon go barefoot as give up kicking. After all, I'd been kicking things practically all my life. Trees, pinecones, tin cans, pebbles; whatever lay in my path, to my way of thinking, deserved a good kick.

Mom said, "I might be able to glue that sole."

I started to hand her my shoe.

She said, "Not now. You need to leave for school. If glue doesn't work ... We've used most of our shoe stamps. There's not a one left in your book."

Being thirteen and wrapped up in my own fun-filled world, I'd paid scant attention to the shortages caused by our country's need for war materials during World War II. Sure, I knew vaguely about having an army to feed and that much of our country's shoe leather went to making combat boots. As had everyone else in the family, I'd been issued a ration book with stamps for meat, sugar, shoes, coffee, and more. Ration books, however, were for parents (specifically moms) to deal with. While Dad found ways to make our gasoline stamps stretch, Mom hung onto our books and handled the rest.

"Watch those feet, Son," Dad called as I started down the hill toward school.

I made it as far as Bobby's house where an assortment of tricycles and bicycles lent evidence to the fact that Bobby's siblings outnumbered my four-kid family two to one. A pop bottle lay among the twigs and wrappers littering the broken sidewalk in front of the old white two-story. Nesbitt orange. My favorite.

I gave the bottle a kick and watched it spin, then gave it another kick. I glanced over my shoulder to see if Dad was looking. He was.

Bobby came outside and I forgot about Dad. We took turns kicking the bottle. We kicked it for four blocks, then five.

"Some girl's gonna tattle if this lands on the school grounds," Bobby said.

I gave the bottle a final kick and sent it spinning into the bushes in front of the house next to the school. Inside, as I took the stairs two at a time to my eighth grade classroom, the rubber band broke.

"What are you going to do now?" Bobby asked.

I shrugged. "I dunno. Get new shoes, I guess." Actually, a flapping shoe sole could be fun.

Two could be more fun. At recess, since my left shoe sole had also started to loosen, I dug my toe into the dirt and loosened it some more. Two flapping soles, and I fancied myself kin to a hobo I'd seen down along the railroad tracks. For the rest of the day, with Bobby egging me on, I flapped in and out of the classroom. Walking home, I entertained Bobby and the rest of my friends with still more flapping.

Since neither parent was apt to break into song over the demise of my left shoe, and my house sat in full view of Bobby's, I quit flapping at the edge of his driveway. But by now, the soles had developed lives of their own. No matter how slowly I plodded across the street and up our front sidewalk, the soles continued to flap.

Mom got out the glue. The soles refused to stick. Dad said he'd take care of it.

Next day, and for several days after, I drug myself to school and even to Sunday school with Dad's flap-stopper invention wrapped around the toe of each shoe. While those tightly tied shoestrings put a stop to my flapping, I had only to get past Bobby's house to resume kicking. Without once thinking of the damage being done to what was left of my shoes, I kicked every rock and mailbox post I came to.

Finally, my older sister, who was in high school and spent a lot of time in front of the mirror, said, "Can't you do anything about Norman's shoes? He looks terrible."

Like most adolescent boys, embarrassing a sister offered scant cause for worry.

The minute Mom left the room, I said, "I told them I needed shoes, and Mom said we don't have any more stamps, so there."

"There's one stamp left. I saw it," my sister argued.

She was right. I had seen the stamp too and knew whose it was.

The next Saturday morning Mom's holler penetrated the aroma of pancakes drifting up the stairs. "Put your school clothes on. We're going to town."

Town? Who wanted to waste a good Saturday going to town? I said as much as I stomped downstairs and settled into my place at the breakfast table.

Mom gave me a look. "You can't try on shoes and play at the same time."

"But you said we don't have any stamps."

"We have one."

"I know. It's Dad's."

She told me to stop arguing and eat my breakfast so we could get going before the stores got busy. She didn't have to tell me twice. Pancakes floating in butter and thick golden molasses go down easy.

An hour later I walked out of Byrd's Shoe Store wearing brand-new shoes. A piece of brick on the sidewalk and assorted trash in the gutter failed to tempt me. I made it to the car without kicking a thing.

The minute we got home I took off my new shoes, set them on my side of the dresser I shared with my brother, and pulled on my old shoes. I leapt downstairs, slammed out of the house, kicked the porch post, the elm tree, and everything else that lay in my path.

Next morning, I woke early. Maybe I'd do something nice for my folks—like set the table without being told—as a thank-you for buying me new shoes. It being my habit to eat Sunday breakfast in my pajamas and dress for church later, I slid out of bed, picked up my new shoes, and tiptoed downstairs.

I didn't see Dad in the kitchen until I was halfway across the dining room. Mom's little radio sat on the buffet and he had it turned on low. The mellow sound of the Blackwood Brothers Quartet filled the space between us. Coincidentally, they were singing, "Take my feet, and let them be Swift and beautiful for Thee" from the old hymn by Frances Havergal, "Take My Life, and Let It Be."

Dad had Mom's scissors in one hand and an empty Wheaties box in the other. As I stood there watching, holding my new shoes, I saw him cut a cardboard oval from the front of the box and use it for a pattern to cut five more. Stacking the ovals together he separated them into two piles. Removing his shoes, he carefully fitted the cardboard into the inside of first one shoe and then the other. A flash of orange told me just how big the holes had gotten to be in the soles of his shoes.

Swallowing hard, I turned and crept back upstairs.

I wish I could say we had only a few days' wait before being issued new ration books replete with shoe stamps. Or that I stopped kicking stuff and quit snickering with my friends over the schlumping sound of a flapping shoe sole. I have no idea how many months passed or how many boxes of Wheaties our family devoured before Dad's need to fill the ever-widening gap in the soles of his shoes came to an end. After all, I was still a kid.

Still, the day I crept back upstairs I knew what I wanted to be like when I grew up. While it took some growing for me to understand and appreciate the sacrifice behind those oval cutouts of orange cardboard, I've tried my best ever since to be like Dad.

Now that I've come to know the Father, who delights to give hugs in the form of good gifts to his children, I think I know my Dad better. I still want to be like the man who first modeled to me the giving nature of my heavenly Father.

THE COMFORT OF A FATHER

LOST IN A CROWD

JUDY HALONE

I was six years old the day Daddy drove me to downtown Portland, Oregon. His '63 Ford pickup looked small when he parked near a tall skyscraper. What a thrill to think we'd soon be whisked away to its top.

We entered the building's lobby and stepped into one of four busy elevators. Piped-in music blended with hushed tones of morning conversations. Scents of aftershave and perfume filled the crowded space. Lights blinked each time we approached another floor, the high-speed car racing upward.

No matter where we went, it seemed that Daddy always happened to know somebody—and even now he'd found a friend to speak with. Their conversation continued while the door opened and closed, with people quickly coming and going.

Then it happened.

Somewhere between the first and thirtieth floors, the familiar *ding!* sounded. I hurried out, staring at an elegant water fountain straight ahead. Activity whirled all around me. From behind, a familiar, deep voice echoed throughout the office.

"Judy!" Daddy's voice—the one I knew better than all others—yelled frantically through the crack of the fast-closing door.

It was too late. I turned around, but he was gone.

The office teemed with activity. Phones rang. Typewriters clicked. Papers shuffled. Employees paced in all directions. No one seemed to notice a misplaced little girl. I stood alone in a crowd.

I dashed toward the nearby elevators. My small fists pounded frantically on the up and down buttons. Two doors suddenly opened at the same time; both were empty. My heart beat heavily in my throat. I could barely breathe. *Where was Daddy?*

Fight-or-flight panic set in. It was impossible to stand still. I needed to find Daddy—now! I fled into one of the elevators, begging its doors to close quickly. Downward I went.

Tears stung my eyes, and my stomach churned. Loneliness filled my young heart. The elevator door finally opened to the ground floor. In front of me, a kindly woman stood waiting to enter.

"I lost my daddy!" I screamed.

The woman's eyebrows arched with concern. She lowered her briefcase and reached for my hand. "Come with me. We'll just stay here for a while."

With a gentle, smooth voice, the woman led me to a nearby desk. She proudly showed a picture of a little girl just about my age with teeth missing in front—just like me.

Her efforts to calm me didn't work well. My heart pulsated in my throat, and my sobs turned into uncontrollable hiccups. Never had I felt so lost.

The elevators' doors repeatedly opened and closed. Each time I heard the familiar *ding!* I glanced up in search of Daddy. But the people who busily entered and exited didn't look like him. I felt like the stray pets I'd seen by the side of the road who longed for just the right car to stop.

The kind woman continued to talk with me, and my breathing quieted a bit. But the immense sense of abandonment did not. I desperately needed Daddy's comfort—his voice, his touch, his presence.

After what must have been a hundred glances toward the elevators, the large silver doors finally opened, and out walked Daddy. How he knew where to find me, I'll never know. But his eyes made immediate contact with me. With one scoop of his arms I was safe once again.

"Daddy! I lost you!" I finally blurted.

Daddy's gentle smile brought a warm comfort and reassurance. He lowered me down and bent eye-level—this man so very tall in my eyes. "Honey, you're Daddy's little girl. You were lost, but I found you." His eyes misted when he tousled my blond hair.

Nearly four decades have passed since the day I was lost, and then found. I'd be lying if I said things ran smoothly between the first and thirtieth floors of my life. But the bells of experience have resounded through many mistakes, poorly made decisions, and heartaches.

Numerous times I've tried hitting the buttons of self-help. But my life only resembled the frenzied office I had inadvertently stepped into. The world quickly raced by, leaving me to feel lost in a crowd.

Then one day I was comforted when I read how Jesus spoke of a lost lamb who longed for the embrace of its shepherd. Sheep may feel alone or lost, but a good shepherd knows right where to look. The lamb never really *was* alone.

And neither am I.

Now when I need comfort, I know there's a choice: I can either hit the buttons of panic, hope for the right doors to open, and run in. Or I can stand still, wait, and know that my Shepherd is on his way to me. He's ready to scoop me into his arms, because that's what my Father does best.

All I have to do is stay put and cry out, "Daddy!"

I know the comfort of his voice, his touch, his presence: *"Honey, you're Daddy's little girl. You were lost, but I found you!"*

THE CAKE BAKE

ROBERT C. PETERSON

My father and I decided to participate in a father-son cake bake. Dad pulled out Mom's large cookbook with the red-and-white checkered cover from the top shelf. Grabbing the step stool, I stood taller as Dad set the book on the counter top. Oil stains and worn edges marked the most used pages. We flipped to the cakes and desserts section, looking for something to show off our soon-to-be-acquired cooking skills.

The pineapple-upside-down cake looked challenging, but neither of us liked pineapple. We looked forward to eating this cake. White cake, chocolate cake, angel food cake, cheesecake—was that really a cake?

Then we saw it—a beautiful twist of yellow and chocolate cake with a fine glaze, a marble cake. That would show how well Dad and I worked together.

We explored the kitchen for the various ingredients, mixing bowls, and spoons to bring this creation to life. Dad and I hadn't done many projects together. Transferring from the security of

Mom's world into the uncharted territory of men, the kitchen provided a safe place to begin.

Standing side by side on Mom's turf, Dad and I mixed, poured, and followed the instructions exactly . . . well, almost. When mixing the dry ingredients—the flour, baking powder, and baking soda—I used a half-tablespoon of salt rather than a half-teaspoon. *What a dummy.* Tears welled.

Dad consoled me, "We will impress those judges with our exquisite delicacy. We just have to start again from the beginning. It's okay, Son."

The second time we followed the instructions more carefully, folding the white and chocolate batters gently together into the pan. No ordinary cake would do. We would create a masterpiece.

The cake baked perfectly; it was small, but beautiful. Head and shoulders back, chest out a bit, a little puffed up like a rooster stepping through the hen house, I felt we had accomplished something great.

That evening the family piled into the car. Mom held the cake for the trip to the local school. We entered the gymnasium, and Mother let me carry the cake. I walked with my head held high. After all, I carried the winning entry, the most delicious cake to enter the room.

As I approached the table I entered another world. A giant green crocodile, a train, and other creations so colorful and coated in layers of frosting, they didn't look like cakes at all. I thought I'd traveled to Candyland. I set my tiny loaf pan down among these sugar monsters and wondered what went wrong. Our little creation did not even have frosting. It was glazed. The others looked more like sculptures for an art show than entries in a cake bake. Was I in the right room? Were those cakes?

With tears in my eyes, I walked to our table. "I think we missed the point."

My dad came over and hugged me. "Son, I'm sorry. I thought it was a baking contest, to test cooking skill. I had no idea it was a cake decorating contest."

It's sometimes hard for a child to understand when communication goes awry. Anger welled up inside me. Why didn't they say cake decorating contest instead of baking contest? Our tiny little baked cake didn't stand a chance against those iced beasts.

I sat down, thinking the worst must be over. *They will hand out the prizes, and I can crawl over, get my cake, and slither out the door.* I consoled myself by imagining the first delicious bite Dad and I would share when we got home. We planned all along to eat our creation. Then they made the most evil announcement, something about auctioning off the cakes after awarding the prizes.

"An auction . . . you mean for money? Dad, you did bring some money, right?"

I turned to see my father checking his pockets. He turned to Mother, who rummaged in her purse. He came and stood behind me. "Son, I didn't know. Your mother and I didn't bring any money. I'm sorry."

I was devastated, and sure things could not get any worse. I dropped into a place of despair that I've never felt before. I felt like the colored train ran me over and the alligator cake ate the remaining pieces with its candy corn teeth. Defeated, I hoped we would just leave.

Dad talked to a few folks. I heard him ask Mother how we could have misunderstood and not known. Everything blurred together. I watched the desperation on my father's face. He turned toward me as he talked to someone in charge. He had a look of guilt and helplessness, like a dog when you catch him wetting on the carpet.

"Son, I'd do anything to fix this, but I can't. I'm sorry." My father put his arm around me and held me.

I saw it in his eyes and felt it in his embrace that he more than shared my pain; he wanted to take it away.

He suffered with me, but if he could have, he would have suffered for me. My father's efforts weren't to save our cake. He was trying to save me.

I realized then the love my father had for me. It hurt him to see me unhappy. With that realization, a warmth covered the hurt in my heart. The cake didn't matter.

My father's comfort showed me how much he loved me. Over the years, his example has helped me understand God the Father's compassion in difficult times.

DISMANTLE YOUR GLORY

TOMMY TENNEY

from *The God Chasers*

The burial of man's glory is the birth of God's glory.

W e have lost the art of adoring the Lord. Our worship gets so cluttered with endless strings of shallow and insincere words that all we do most of the time is "take up space" or "put in prayer time" with a passionless monologue that even God must ignore.

Some of us come to Him clinging to such heavy burdens that we are too frustrated and distracted to see the Father or understand how much He loves us. We need to return to the simplicity of our childhood. Every night that I'm home, I rock my six-year-old daughter to sleep because I love her. Usually she will lie back in my arms, and just before she drifts off to sleep she will remember the problems of the day and say something like, "Daddy, this little boy was mean to me on the playground at school," or "Daddy, I had trouble on my spelling test today." To her these seem like giant problems. I always try to reassure her that everything will be all right in those moments because she is resting in my arms and because I love her. It doesn't matter what anyone said on the playground, and none of her little failures have any power to hurt her because she is in my arms.

Somehow, when I'm able to weave my way through the labyrinth of a six-year-old mind and bring peace to her, I get to enjoy my favorite part of the day. That is when my little girl just lays her head back to look at me with her eyes half open and give me her little smile. The only way I know to describe it is that her face displays sheer adoration and complete security in those moments. She doesn't have to speak; I understand. And then in complete peace she drifts off to sleep with the smile of safety and trust on her face.

God wants us to do the same thing. Too often we come to Him at the end of our day and "worship" Him with premanufactured mechanics and memorized words. Then, since we are almost totally absorbed with our "playground" offenses and the temporal problems of the day, we lie back in His presence just long enough to say our string of words and deliver our wish list. Then we jump up and run off to continue our frustrated rat-race lives. Often we never seem to find that place of perfect peace.

What He wants us to do is just look at Him. Yes, we can tell Him what we feel. We need to tell Him, but He is really waiting to receive our most intimate worship and adoration, the kind that transcends mere words or outward actions. He has set before you an open door, but you will have to "face" Him. You cannot back your way into the door of eternity; you have to walk into it. You will have to stop looking at and listening to other things. He is beckoning to you to "come up hither," and He'll show you the "hereafter" (see Rev. 4:1 KJV). That should bring peace to a weary child.

$\mathcal{N}$EVER ALONE

BRENDA HENRY

Chaos spilled from every classroom and forced its way into the hallway where I stood cowering beside the drinking fountain. Gigantic eighth graders shoved their way past my six-year-old frame, leaving the impression that the snowstorm outside had entered our school. Shouts of "Where's my mitten?" and "Who took my headband?" echoed through the hall and overwhelmed me.

Scared, I leaned against the painted concrete wall and sank to the floor. As my position lowered, my fear heightened when an ideal view of the blizzard came into view through the large windows on the school's front door. Each time the door opened, the howling wind sounded its warning, slammed the door against the inside wall, and allowed anxious parents in to bundle up and deliver their child safely home.

With every slam of the doorknob against the wall and every unfamiliar face that entered, my knees, held tight by my arms, drew closer to my chin. Remaining stranded at school in the middle of a blizzard was unthinkable. My thoughts spun around in my head like the whirlwind outside the school. *Who will come for me? Mom's afraid of snowstorms. She can't drive in this. She'll never make it. Dad's at work. There's no one. What will happen to me?*

Petrifying fear of being left alone with the "mean" teachers kept me seated below the coat hooks. I fixed my eyes on the foyer door, knowing it was the only entry point for any potential hero to reach me. I wished the shouting and bustling would drown out my thoughts, but their aggressive efforts pushed in on me, leaving me impotent to calm down. Pressed against the wall as scarves and boots flew past my head, I felt alone. I was cold, I was frightened, and I was missing one mitten. I just wanted to go home ... *but who would come for me?*

Then, through the frosty glass in the front doors, I saw Dad bounding up the stairs. My buckled knees did an about-face and held me as I jumped to my feet. By the time he turned the knob and the wind slammed the door open on my behalf, I'd already shouted "Dad's here!" three times. Fear melted away like the snowflakes he brushed off his jacket. As I watched his piercing blue eyes sweep the room for me, I realized he'd never leave me alone. He wouldn't even consider it.

When our eyes finally locked, mine brimmed with tears. Relief filled me, but my knees remained locked and my feet wouldn't budge. He did not take his eyes from me as he strode toward me through the thinning crowd of students. Stooping down beside me, he removed his gloves, wiped my wet cheek, and whispered, "You ready?"

My spindly arms reached toward him.

Safe in his strong arms, my head bobbed above the remaining kids as he carried me toward the exit. He gave me one last reassuring look before wrestling with the school door, and then he stepped into the storm.

Once outside, he set me down, grabbed my mittenless hand, and we sprinted across the blustery street together. Secure inside his old white pickup, we brushed ourselves off and buckled up. Dad winked at me and put the truck into gear. I rested my head on his shoulder and allowed the relief to sink in. The storm swelled outside the dented truck, but I felt safe inside the cab, sitting next to Dad.

Even though that event took place many years ago, I've never forgotten that stormy day and Dad's rescue. It reminds me that my heavenly Father has already done the same. He is ready to help at a moment's notice and no matter what the circumstance, he wouldn't even consider leaving me alone.

Remembering the fear and loneliness I felt as I shivered against the unyielding cinder-block wall of my grade school, I see him enter our noisy world, fraught with chaos and distraction. I sense him finding me, stooping down beside me and, as his piercing eyes search mine, I hear him say, "Good news, kiddo. I'm here. You ready?"

"Are you the One?" I ask, "Are you the One to carry me home?"

He nods. I reach toward him, grip his hand tightly, and feel him lift me up. Walking beside him, I am aware that the cold in my fingertips has disappeared, replaced by pervasive warmth that permeates all the way to my heart.

Abba, I think, *I knew you'd come.*

A FATHER'S FELLOWSHIP

BUILDING BLOCKS

MIKE MASON

from *The Mystery of Children*

Heather is ten, it's a Sunday afternoon, and she and I carry a pile of sports equipment up to the park near our house. We've got a bat and ball, a Frisbee, a basketball, tennis and badminton rackets, and an old red Australian football that I love. At this age, rather than staying with one activity, Heather likes to sample a bit of everything.

My Australian football won't hold much air anymore, so it's soft enough not to knock Heather's head off. She still lacks confidence when it comes to catching or throwing balls. For years she wouldn't touch the football, but now we're tossing it around and she's doing pretty well. Every time she catches it, she looks surprised, as if the ball had come to her because it liked her.

After a while we make up some simple plays. I hike to her, drop back for a handoff, then she goes for a short pass or rolls out to the side for a lateral. We do fakes, zigzags, buttonhooks. My favorite play, of course, is the Long Bomb. But I know she's not ready for that.

Even so, just for fun, as we're in the huddle with our arms draped around each other's shoulders, I say, "Okay, Heath, it's time for the Long Bomb."

"The what?"

"The Long Bomb. You hike to me, then run like a jackrabbit as far as you can go. Don't look back until you hear me yell, then turn around and put up your arms, and the ball will be right there."

"How far should I go?"

"Far. Farther than you can believe. And don't worry. When I yell, you turn around and the ball will just be sitting there in the air like it's on a shelf just above your ear. All you have to do is reach up and nab it."

So Heather snaps the ball and starts loping out down the long field. How far should I let her go? I'm not even sure how far I can throw this thing anymore. But I feel the sweet, smooth adrenaline flowing into my arm and out to my fingertips, and I sense the same gorgeous stuff coursing through my daughter too, connecting us by an invisible cord as we both imagine her with fingers of sandpaper and arms that can reach out and encircle any star.

Once, just once, she looks back, wondering if I still exist, not believing I could possibly mean this far. But I yell, "No, no—not yet—keep on going—way down there—way-y-y-y-y-y-y dowwwwwwwwn there . . ."

So she keeps on going until finally something tells me, some mysterious signal, that this is it, this is the moment, and I lean back against the wind, one arm stretched forward and one way back, front toe barely touching the ground, and then I let fly that soaring star, launch it like a missile and can almost hear it whistling through the air, homing to its mark, while in my bones I'm wanting, wishing, willing my daughter to catch it, picturing it live and kicking in her hands, a red leather bomb still moving like fury but yielding to her if only she'll tighten her grip around it like a cat's jaws into a bird's throat until she has it, has it for ever and ever, bringing it tight against her body until no one can take it away from her, no one can ever take that moment away.

And that's when I yell: "OKAY, HEATHER!" And as she turns around, sure enough the ball is right there, right on the money, hanging beside her ear like an apple that, as she reaches for it, seems to turn into a bird and float right into her hands. And then she has it. Tight against her body. For ever and ever. YES!

For a moment, bewildered, she looks back at me in disbelief, peers back at the tiny figure of her father way down at the other end of the field, such a long, long distance away. And then she explodes. She jumps straight up in the air and cheers and then starts running toward me, and I run toward her, and we're both running and jumping and yelling with all the joy that's fountaining up from deep inside us into our throats and mouths and spilling out all over that great gigantic field.

My daughter, ten years old, has just caught the longest pass her old man can throw, and as we rush into each other's arms, the field, the whole earth, moves under our feet, spins with love.

Editor's Note: At times, our heavenly Father sends his children on an adventure. Separated by distance and time, we look back, questioning if he meant for us to travel this far alone. But when he determines we've gone just the right distance, he sends his spirit to meet us. At the sound of his voice we turn and he is there. The prize is near; we reach out and gather it into our arms. At last we understand. And together we rejoice.

$\mathcal{A}$LONGSIDE MY FATHER

NANCY HIRD

M y ten-year-old mind could see it—a sweet pink cloud on a paper cone. Umm-m ... cotton candy. I licked my lips and made a little bounce on the backseat of our car. I could hardly wait. We were going to the fair. My family and I were going to spend the whole summer afternoon there. We were going to eat cotton candy and ride the Ferris wheel and see the Dancing Waters. We were going to—

Daddy turned to Mom. "Does the car feel like it's leaning to the left?" He stuck his head out of the front side window, and I stuck my head out the back. "I can hear thumping," he said and sighed. He pulled the car over to the curb and all six of us got out. Daddy walked around the car and then shook his head in disgust. "The left rear tire is flat," he said.

"You can fix it, can't you, Daddy?" I asked nervously. I could feel the afternoon ticking away.

"Well, I could if we had a spare in the trunk, but we don't," he said.

He looked as disappointed as I felt. He also looked worried. Tires cost money and my family had little extra.

"What are we going to do?" I asked.

Daddy ran a large, strong hand through his thinning brown hair. Then he smiled. It was a brilliant smile as if he had just thought of the most wonderful joke. "We'll go home and I'll get a tire off the old car and put it on this one." He was referring to the old broken-down car that he had parked on the side of our house. That car didn't run anymore and most people would have hauled it away to the junkyard, but Daddy said it was stupid to throw away good parts.

Mom found a pay phone and called a neighbor who came to get us. Dragging my feet, I got into the neighbor's car; the day was ruined. We weren't going to the fair.

At home it took Daddy a while to take the tire off the old car. I watched out of the corner of my eye. I wouldn't turn my head and watch him full faced. I was so disappointed. Instead, I dug my feet deeper into the grass and sulked. Daddy rolled the tire past me and down the street.

Suddenly, he stopped and turned. "Do you want to come?" he asked.

No, I thought, staring at the ground. *Who'd want to walk two long, boring miles? And just to fix a tire?*

"Go with him," Mom urged. "Just to keep him company."

I squirmed and made a face, but one look at her set mouth told me I wasn't going to win this argument. *Okay*, I thought, *I'll go, but I'm not going to like it.* I gave her one last protesting frown—just to remind her I wasn't a pushover—and then, shrugging, trotted off to where Daddy waited.

The corners of his mouth turned up in a soft smile and his blue eyes shone with welcome. With his broad hands he gave the black rubber tread a shove, and we were off.

After a couple of blocks he asked, "Would you like a turn?"

I hesitated, but he gave me such a grin that I nodded.

So taking turns, we pushed that tire past houses and down country roads. We moved silently at first because I was still in a grump. But rolling the tire turned out to be fun, and before long I was talking Daddy's ear off. Much too soon we came to our stranded car.

Now for the boring part, I thought. *A whole half hour with nothing to do.* I plopped down on the curb and stared into space.

"Come here," Daddy said.

Why? I thought. But I wanted to please him so I rose and walked to him.

"This is a jack," he said, holding out a metal bar. He fitted it into a metal stand that lay on the ground beneath the rear bumper. "I'm only going to lift the car a little right now," he explained, pushing down on the jack handle, "just enough to take the weight off the tire."

Then coming around he popped off the hubcap and with the tire iron began to loosen a nut. I could see that nuts don't come off easily because he clenched his teeth and screwed his face tight with the effort. But the nut was no match for Daddy. It gave; his face relaxed, and he twirled the iron on its axis like a baton. "Here," he said, "you do it."

I hesitated. It looked hard.

"Come on," he coaxed, smiling reassuringly. Gently, he placed my hands on the iron. Then he put his hands over mine and together we slowly turned the iron. After a couple of rounds, he took his hands away and stepped back. He nodded to me to continue. I took a breath and slowly began turning the iron on my own. The nut got looser. I was amazed. I was actually doing it. Soon the nut was ready to come off and I dropped it triumphantly into the hubcap. Oh, it made a merry clink.

Daddy started another nut and then, stepping back, let me twist that one off too. I felt so proud, so happy. I was helping my dad.

When we finished changing the tire, Daddy looked at me and smiled a smile that nearly cracked his face. "Thanks for helping," he said. "Thanks for coming along and keeping me company."

I beamed back at him. I just beamed. I felt as if I were riding the clouds. Not for a whole month of days at the fair would I have traded that afternoon with him.

When I sense God asking me to walk with him, I often think about that afternoon with my dad. Like him, God could do the work by himself, but he too invites me to come along. He will do the hard parts and I will learn from him and about him. David says of walking with God, "You have made known to me the path of life; you will fill me with joy in your presence, with eternal pleasures at your right hand" (Ps. 16:11).

COME AND FISH

SHARON HINCK

"Let's go fishing."

Each time my dad gave that invitation, my heart raced like a lure flashing through the water. My most evocative memories of Dad center on afternoons of waiting for the Big One to bite. The sound of an outboard motor and the slap of waves against an aluminum hull can still raise my pulse.

As I grew up I cherished each rare fishing trip. Dad was an on-the-go executive who traveled a lot. But when we fished, we both surrendered to the peace of a sun-soaked Minnesota lake. It was our special time. Anticipation built while I watched my bobber float and listened to ducks calling to each other in the reeds. When my rod gave an exhilarating tug, I relished the battle of reeling in a sunfish, no matter how tiny the catch.

Dad would congratulate me and add the fish to our stringer. Then he'd tell me about the huge northern pike and walleye he caught on his fishing trips in Canada. He promised that when I was older, he'd take me along one day for some serious fishing.

But years swam past. I struggled with adolescence. He battled cancer. Sometimes we fought each other.

I left for college, got engaged, and my fiancé became the primary man in my life. The next summer, home for vacation, I sat at the kitchen counter making a cheese sandwich. Dad came in from cleaning the garage and poured himself a glass of buttermilk.

I spread mayonnaise on my bread. "So, Dad. Next summer I'll be married."

He nodded. "Yep. Hard to believe."

"And we never took that big fishing trip together."

He set his glass down. "You still like fishing?"

"It's been a while. But, yeah. I still want to try my hand at landing a northern."

He rubbed his hand over his crew cut and cleared his throat. "Let's do it."

That weekend we made the long drive north to Lake of the Woods on the Canadian border. We rented a musty cabin and stocked up on Kit Kats and Coke. The next morning we headed out through predawn mist on our quest to do some serious fishing.

The scent of gasoline from the motor mingled with the tang of Coppertone—an alluring combination that promised adventure.

We motored along the shore and stopped in promising coves to cast for a while. My lure kept tangling in the weeds. Dad patiently helped me pull it free so I could cast again.

By the time the sun was fully up I felt my first strike. I cranked and played the fish while Dad coached me. The northern pike was a more demanding foe than the sunfish and perch of my youth. I teased it closer to the boat, and Dad stood up with the net. The boat rocked. My rod arced from the strain. Dad swooped the net, and a long, gleaming pike flopped into the bottom of our boat.

"This one's a beauty," Dad said.

It was a proud moment. Dad had invited me into his world and

I proved I could catch the big ones, just like he did. Suddenly Dad's fishing rod jumped, and it was my turn to grab the net. I helped him land his catch, and the fish kept us busy the rest of the afternoon.

I still have the photo that Dad took of me at the end of our day of fishing. In the snapshot I'm wearing a stained bandana over my hair and a red flannel shirt. My nose is pink from not using enough sunscreen. I'm holding a stringer of northern pike that I could barely lift, and my grin is so huge it makes my eyes squint.

That was the last fishing trip Dad and I took together. The next summer he walked me down the aisle at my wedding. Three years later he lost his battle with cancer.

That day of fishing stands out in my mind as a perfect memory of Dad. He shared one of his greatest pleasures with me and let me see his pride in me—things that reflected God's love in my life.

Dad showed his love the best way he could. He took me fishing. Because of those times, I know how wonderful it feels to have my Father in the boat with me. He may have to bait my hook and untangle my line. But he still smiles on me with pleasure. And I learned the power of that kind of love from my dad.

ALONG FOR THE RIDE

SANDRA WOOD

O ne of Dad's favorite ways to spend leisure time is to get in his blue pickup truck and go somewhere he's never visited on a road that few people travel. Afterward, he faithfully marks his route with a yellow highlighter on a large wall map to record the journey. This system reminds Dad never to take the same journey twice. Tucked into his memory are thousands of hours of yellow-brick-road trips and knowledge about the terrain, the obstacles, and the extraordinary views along the highways of our country.

Some of my most cherished memories are those I spent in the passenger seat next to Dad when he offered to repeat his favorite routes and to share the sights and sounds that delighted him. In the silence and in the stories, we relished the past, considered the present, and debated future possibilities. Each day's journey led to a better understanding of each other's heart.

This year, my career ended abruptly after twenty-four years of service and I was left without a clear road map for the second half of my life. I decided to spend extra time with my parents at Flathead

Lake, Montana. In the stillness of every sunrise, I experienced the birth of hope. In the surrender of every sunset, I felt God's peace. And in the midst of a life transition, I found time to live life abundantly—to rest and play and join my dad on one of his favorite road trips.

After weeks of exploring Goose Bay and the surrounding towns by foot, we set out on a truck ride into the surrounding mountains and forests. We packed a cooler with diet cola and set out without a specific route or agenda. I packed my camera to record the memories. He packed a cell phone to call home periodically.

With Dad at the wheel, my natural fear of heights almost disappeared and we drove to the top of many roads I would never have ventured alone. There at the top of the world, I could see for miles. Along the way, his trained eyes spotted two deer on their way to drink from a nearby stream. He called out so I would not miss the sight. I asked him to slow down for a photo. In my imagination I could hear him groan, but in the cabin of the truck I could only hear him chuckle.

"You know, deer are known as forest rabbits by the locals around here," Dad said. "They are as fast as rabbits and multiply just like them."

"Be quiet and stop the truck," I replied, and watched him smile.

We bumped along dirt roads that were rutted by the weight of the logging trucks and weather extremes. On all sides of the road, for as far as my eyes could see, there were trees. Evergreen and deciduous trees blanketed the rugged mountains. Green complemented green with countless shades of color. Forests bloomed with wild flowers in yellow, red, purple, and orange.

Dad slowed the truck to accommodate my interest and pointed out how to tell a fir tree from a cedar tree from a tamarack tree. He briefly pointed out the standing dead trees that were fair game for firewood, but asked me not to dwell too long. He didn't want me to miss the life of the forest. We enjoyed each other's company and narrowed our focus from mountaintop, to treetop, to flower petal.

Dad's eyes focused on the horizon and the bends in the road. "Look," Dad said. "There's a black bear in the road."

I knew if I tried to focus my camera to capture the moment I would miss the enjoyment of watching the animal. I sat upright and shouted.

"Wow! What if he had come just a few moments earlier when I was shooting a picture of the flower? What should I do in that case, Dad?"

In a typical Dad-like answer he replied, "Well, that depends. . . ." He followed up by adding "Usually, bears are more afraid of you than you are of them. Stand still and wait for him to run."

The rattle of the truck bed was our only music. Conversation was light. I rode for hours in the presence of my father and realized how much fun it was to be with him. In the safety of the moment I wanted to know him better. Did I dare break the moment with a more personal question about our future relationship as father and daughter?

"If money were no object, would you want your grown children to live with you forever?" I asked.

I was interested in hearing his response because as a single adult I live in my parents' home. Half of each year, we live together in their home in California. The other half, they spend at their home in Montana. As I considered alternatives for my future, I wanted to know if I could assume I would be welcome in their home.

"If money were no object, it wouldn't matter. We'd have plenty of homes," he answered with wry humor.

"Okay, I'll ask it another way. Do you ever think about what it would be like to have your children live with you forever? Do you think you would mind?"

Without taking his eyes off the road, without a moment's hesitation, Dad answered.

"You kids have become our friends and we love having you around. Our home is your home for as long as you need our help."

In that response, Dad's love mirrored the love of our heavenly Father. Our truck ride was a picture of how God wants to travel through life with us. Dad was at the wheel during our drive and that was fine with me. He showed me paths and took me places I didn't know existed. He led me beyond limits I set for myself so I could view the extraordinary. He shared his favorite roads and went at my pace, so I didn't miss any of the details. The destination wasn't as important to him as the route we took to get there. He stopped frequently so I could touch, taste, and smell life. Together, my dad and I experienced joy in the simple presence of each other.

God the Father desires the same.

God created us for companionship and would like to take each of us for the ride of our life. He wants us to explore routes that few people have traveled. He promises to show us new, unimaginable things. He warns us that the road may be bumpy at times, but we needn't worry. God is behind the wheel.

We may not know the destination, but the Father does. He wants us to go with him, to see what he has created. He wants us to share undivided time with him and ask him impossible questions. He wants us to know that we are his children and his friends. He has prepared a home with many rooms, and he intends to share it with us forever. When we decide to ride along with our heavenly Father, the journey will never be routine. We may meet few other travelers on the narrow back roads, but we will never lack companionship.

Sometime, during the ride, Father God may drape his arm over the back of our seat and ask, "Is there somewhere else you dream to go?" If we will surrender to the embrace and the whim of the driver, he will show us the path of life and fill us with joy in his presence.

$\mathscr{N}$IGHTMARE IN SECOND GRADE

———— ◆ ————

PHIL CALLAWAY

—◦ from *I Used to Have Answers, Now I Have Kids* ◦—

I suppose it all began way back in second grade when Miss Barzley came to town. Before Miss Barzley I didn't know how to spell terror. But after her first visit, the very sight of that white Health Department cruiser was enough to send our entire class scattering for seclusion in the nearby woods.

"I just saw The Car," Leslie Kolibaba would whisper, horror etched on his seven-year-old face. And we would tremble and clutch our arms and moan softly.

It wasn't always this way. The first time Miss Barzley came to town, we trusted her entirely. And so, like very young lambs, we were lined up single file in a darkened hallway and shot one by one.

I remember standing for the very first time near the back of the line, unsure of the results of reaching the front. Those who had gone on ahead were filing by with "attempted amputation" written all over their voices. "OOOOWWWW!" was how they put it, as they rolled down their sleeves. Oh, how I longed for the hand of my father. He would show Miss Barzley.

But each of us entered The Room dreadfully alone.

Miss Barzley was a rather imposing figure, even without the needle in her hand. Large storehouses of fat (we nicknamed them Lester and Bob) hung like butterballs from her arms as she lifted them upward, squinting at the needle, and squeezing a few drops heavenward. Her smile was screwed tightly shut on her humorless face. The glasses on her nose were the thickest I'd ever seen, and she reminded me of a huge insect, a mosquito, I suppose. "Roll up your sleeve. It won't hurt," Miss Barzley lied. Then she poked us. It took just a moment, but we were scarred for life.

Once she finished, she handed me a sugar cube, the reward for not passing out. I tried to take two, but she spotted me with her big eyes and squashed me like a bug.

Twenty-three years later, when my wife informed me that the time had arrived for our son, Stephen, to receive the shot some adult members of our civilized society have decided to give all five-year-olds, I volunteered to take him to the nurse. I was, after all, the obvious choice to comfort him. Having been poked myself, I knew what he was facing. I would hold his hand. Cringe with him. It's something brave fathers do these days.

"Will it hurt, Daddy?" We were on our way to the clinic now, and I had just informed my son of the reason. The tears came quickly as the news shattered his gentle world of cowboy games and toy guns.

"Well son," I said, remembering an old lie told me by a young dentist, "it will pinch a little."

"But what will they do?"

"They will put the needle into your arm, and it will come out at your knee."

"Naw," he laughed and began to wipe his tears. Anything Dad jokes about can't be too serious.

"If you are brave, we'll go out for a treat after."

It was enough, for the moment. But upon our arrival, events took a turn for the worse. Unlike the hallway of my experience, our surroundings were pleasant. And the nurse was slender and kind. But the needle was much the same shape of those decades ago, and Stephen was terrified.

Incentives to bravery were offered him: pencils that smell nice (as if children need another reason to chew them), stickers, a coloring book, more stickers, no-charge checking, retirement savings plans—anything, JUST RELAX, PLEASE! But he wouldn't relax, and at last the nurse asked me to hold the horrified child tight as she delivered the goods.

A month has passed. The pain has subsided, but not the memory. Today we are on our way to another clinic. Today we will have our warts removed—together. It seems fear is not the only thing he has inherited.

"What will they do?" asks Stephen.

"They will probably have to take our feet off to work on the warts," answers his dad.

"Naw," he laughs.

"Tell you what, son. I'll be there. Remember, I've got a wart, too. And if we are real brave," I say, "we will get a treat after."

At the clinic, Stephen is terrified again. My presence brings little comfort, my words even less. After all, I was of little help during the last encounter. Why should this be any different?

In the doctor's office we wait. The seasons come and go. Finally the doctor arrives with a bubbling vat of something.

"Sorry I'm late," he says.

"That's okay ... are you sure there isn't something else you should be doing?"

Stephen is looking at the bubbling vat. His eyes are very wide. Like an insect.

"It's liquid nitrogen," says the doc. "Minus three hundred degrees."

Oh good, he's going to freeze our feet off.

"You go first, Phil."

"Uh, me? Um, okay, Doctor."

Slowly I remove my sock. He dips a long Q-Tip into the vat and rubs it on my wart. A little boy watches nervously, his eyes darting between my false smile and my afflicted foot. "See, son, it's gonna be okay."

When Stephen's turn arrives, he is relatively calm. He looks into my face as the doctor dips the Q-Tip. *Daddy can handle it,* the boy is thinking, *so can I.*

Minutes later, we are seated in a nearby restaurant. Our feet are a little tender, but our spirits are good. It's time for our "above and beyond the call of bravery" awards. We have selected the chocolate and raspberry variety. When they arrive, a little boy has some questions.

"Will our warts stay gone?"

"I think so."

"Did yours hurt?"

"A little bit."

"Mine hurt a lot ... but you were there."

As we lick the last of the berries and ice cream, I tell him of Miss Barzley. Of waiting in a darkened hallway to get poked. Of her wobbly arms. Of her big eyes. And of the sharp needles. "Sometimes

I wished my Dad could be there with me, Stephen."

Stephen has run out of ice cream and is eyeing the pop machine.

"Are you glad Daddy was there today?" I ask him.

"Yep." And then he adds, "I'm glad you got poked."

A door opened today. And I saw God in the words of my son. Because, you see, as much as I have marveled at the reality of Jesus Christ's presence in my life; as much as I have been comforted by His reassuring words; never before had I realized exactly why His suffering means so much to me.

God will never take us where He has not been.

As Isaiah put it, "He was pierced for our transgressions, he was crushed for our iniquities; the punishment that brought us peace was upon him, and by his wounds we are healed" (Isaiah 53:5).

Perhaps Stephen would say, "I'm glad He was poked."

Me too. And because of it, nothing will haunt us that He has not handled. Because He conquered death and fear and pain, we can look an uncertain future in the face. Because He was pierced, we have peace.

Whether you're standing in a hospital ward, in an empty house, or at the back of the line in a long, dark hallway, it's worth smiling about.

TRUSTING A FATHER

$\mathscr{M}$Y DADDY IS GOOD

T R A C I E   P E T E R S O N

—— from *The Eyes of the Heart* ——

I sat in the airport the other day waiting for a connecting flight home. I was tired, but the trip had been a real blessing, and so it was a good tired. The kind that comes from a sense of deep satisfaction.

As I sat there waiting, I found myself watching people once again. It was only moments before a uniformed flight attendant came up with a child in hand. The girl looked to be no more than nine or ten. She had lovely chocolate brown eyes, black hair, and the sweetest smile.

"Sit here," the attendant instructed. "I'll come and get you when it's time for the flight."

The girl nodded and took the seat beside mine.

"Don't worry, now," the attendant said with a smile. "I'll just be standing right over here. I'll be able to see you the entire time." The girl nodded and began to swing her legs back and forth.

I smiled at the girl as well. I told her my name and broke the rule about talking to strangers. I figured she was safe. I told her I was heading home after being gone almost a week. I told her that I had a little boy her age. She waited politely for me to finish, all the while swinging her legs. She told me her name and then added that she was traveling from Texas to Missouri to see her sister.

I was so compelled by this girl's ease. She seemed completely content to be traveling alone. Perhaps she had done this numerous times, I thought. Perhaps this was an old routine that she'd grown up with. I decided to ask.

"Do you travel by yourself a lot?"

She shook her head and grinned an infectious grin that warmed my heart. "Nope, this is my first time."

I was impressed. "Are you afraid?" I asked, thinking that if she was, I could offer her some kind of encouragement or conversation until she was on her way once again. Little did I know that she would be the one to offer encouragement.

"Nope. I'm not afraid. My daddy told me things before I got on the airplane."

I was intrigued. What things had her father said that so easily put her at rest about this trip? I hated to pry, but I needed to know. I've been flying for a good part of my adult life, and I'm still not at ease as much as this child.

"So what did your daddy tell you?" I asked.

She gave a little bouncing momentum to her leg swinging. "He told me I didn't need to be afraid. He told me everything would be okay."

I nodded, trying to encourage her confidence, but she needed no encouraging. "He sounds like a very good daddy."

She nodded in rhythm to the bounce and swing. She was a body in perpetual motion. "He is a good daddy," she declared. "He loves me."

She said it with such confidence that I was thinking about her long after the attendant led her away for her next flight.

Her words reminded me of my heavenly Daddy. He too is a good daddy. The best of fathers. And He loves me. I couldn't help but think of the girl's confidence in this now distant man. He had told her she didn't need to be afraid, that everything would be okay.

Joshua 1:9 came to mind: "Have I not commanded you? Be strong and courageous. Do not be terrified; do not be discouraged, for the Lord your God will be with you wherever you go."

Our Daddy says we don't have to be afraid. We don't have to be terrified.

Is something scaring you? Are you trembling in fear, uncertain of the future? Maybe the bills are all due next week or even today, and there's no money in the bank to cover them. Maybe you've prayed and prayed for healing, but the tests keep indicating a problem.

Perhaps someone is threatening you—hovering nearby to cause you harm. Maybe someone wants to see you fired ... evicted ... divorced ... dead. You're afraid to answer the door for fear of who might be on the other side.

"Be strong and courageous ... do not be terrified." Our Daddy is good. He loves us.

Do you believe that? Do you have the faith of a child who upon boarding a plane for a cross-country trip takes the words of her father to heart and has no fear? A child who fairly dances in her seat in anticipation of the journey ahead, even though she is making it alone for the first time?

"Do not be discouraged."

The problems of this world are temporary. Like dust in the wind—momentarily stirred up and then blown away. Our Father promises us that He will be with us wherever we go. He promises us that we don't have to make the journey alone.

Our Daddy is good. He loves us. Take it from the heart of a child who knows. Take it to heart and know for yourself. There will always be problems and conflicts. There will always be things that threaten our balance, our hope. But God is good. He's told us some things before we ever started the journey. He's given us words of wisdom—measures of advice—love letters in His Holy Word.

That little girl helped me to remember that faith is knowing who you're dealing with. She knew her daddy. Her nine or ten years of dealing with him gave her confidence in his behavior and credibility. When he told her it would be okay, she knew she could trust the matter to be right. She knew it because she trusted the one who spoke the words.

Do you trust the one who spoke the Word? Can you have the hope in your heavenly Father that this child had in her earthly one?

Listen. Our Daddy is speaking. He's telling us things . . . things we can take with us . . . things that will help us on our journey.

Are you listening?

Maybe you should take a seat for this one. Grab a copy of the Bible. Cross your legs at the ankle and start swinging them. Now give a little bounce.

Your Daddy loves you . . . and . . . He's got some things to tell you.

JUST WAIT

DR. CHARLES HARREL

A quick look into my room would have given the impression I was fast asleep. Instead, I was hiding under the blankets, scanning a travel brochure with my flashlight. In a few hours we would leave for a vacation at my favorite place: Palomar.

Palomar Mountain State Park in Southern California offered my family the perfect getaway, with its majestic sugar pines, trips to the observatory, and fish that were always hungry. The best camping spot was the one closest to Doane's Pond, where I only had a short hike to the fishing hole. This little pond provided the best trout fishing I'd ever seen. That's what my dad always said, and I agreed with him. We always filled our stringers when we fished at Palomar.

My parents allowed me to explore by myself as long as they could see my location. Besides, there was no way to get lost. We could view the trail, our campsite, and the pond from any angle. Although I was only seven at the time, I couldn't have felt more secure.

One afternoon I rushed down to the fishing hole to stake out a good spot before the evening crowd showed up. I had made the trip from the campsite a dozen times without any problems, so I hardly needed to look twice. Catching a limit of fish was easy for a disciplined angler like me. My Eagle Claw pole and Mitchell reel assured my success. With luck, I would return in thirty minutes.

About the time I should have passed the meadow, I realized something was wrong. The pond was nowhere in sight. When I glanced over my shoulder, the campground had disappeared as well. Now I had a problem. I was lost!

I knew better than to keep walking. My father had always said, "If you ever get lost, just stay where you are and wait. I will be there directly." Using a nearby post as a backrest, I sat down and waited. I was still waiting as the sun dipped low on the horizon and the evening chill crept in. Finally, a forest ranger drove by in his patrol truck; he stopped in front of me. "Hey kid, have you seen a boy about your age?" he asked. "He's missing and his family is worried about him."

Smiling back at the ranger, I shook my head in a silent "No." Before I could think of anything else to say, the pickup rambled down the road and disappeared into a trail of dust. Since I considered myself lost already, it was fortunate the ranger didn't enlist my help with the search. Still, I wondered why he never asked if I was the boy for whom he was searching.

It was almost dark when a big man rounded the corner with a slow but steady pace. It was Dad. My father came looking for me just as he said he would. I felt so secure that night as we headed back to camp, his arm wrapped tightly around my shoulder.

I found out later that the forest ranger didn't believe anyone could get lost sitting by a signpost that read *Doane Valley Campground*. My dad only grinned when he saw me under the sign pointing the way back to our campsite. He never laughed or embarrassed me, because I had patiently waited as he instructed.

Many years have passed since that day. Even as an adult I feel spiritually lost at times, but I always know God will come looking for me. The Bible says that God seeks those who are lost. So whenever I feel helpless or unsure of my next move, I stop for a moment and wait.

God will be there directly.

TRUSTING PAPA

T A M A R A   B O G G S

from *And Then God Gave Us Kids*

So do not fear, for I am with you;
do not be dismayed, for I am your God.
I will strengthen you and help you;
I will uphold you with my righteous right hand.
—ISAIAH 41:10

My help comes from the Lord,
the Maker of heaven and earth.
He will not let your foot slip—
he who watches over you will not slumber;
indeed, he who watches over Israel
will neither slumber nor sleep.
—PSALM 121:2–4

I strode through the house, headed to the backyard with my blow-dryer. My father had taught me the trick of using a blow-dryer to get a charcoal fire going. It looked odd, but always got the job done in a hurry—and I was in a hurry. The guests for my niece's wedding rehearsal dinner were arriving, and I needed to get the food on the table.

Hannah, our nine-month-old, fussed as I passed by the living room. I'd left her in Aunt Susan's capable hands, but Aunt Susan lived out of state and Hannah had only been with her once before. So Hannah wasn't as sure as I was about Aunt Susan's qualifications. But I had to get this fire going, even if Hannah yowled in protest. I walked on through the kitchen and out the back door.

Guests were milling about the yard, talking. I turned on the blow-dryer. A red glow and then orange flames rewarded me. Aunt Susan appeared at the back door, Hannah squirming in her arms. I shut off the wonder dryer.

Hannah put out her arms as Susan came near.

"All right. Come here." I picked up Hannah and she patted my cheek with a chubby hand as if scolding me for leaving her with a stranger.

"Sorry, Susan," I said. "I guess Hannah doesn't know you very well yet."

"That's okay," said Susan. "She'll get to know me better as she gets older."

I went back inside, balancing Hannah on my hip. "Let's see— the buns, condiments, and chips are out on the table. I almost for- got—lettuce and tomato."

Sally, the bride-to-be, walked into the kitchen. "Is there anything I can do to help?"

"I need some slicing done. But, I hate to keep you in here when your friends are outside. How about if you take Hannah out and I'll finish up."

"Sure." Sally put her arms out and smiled at Hannah. Hannah leaned into my chest.

"Come on, Hannah, you know Cousin Sally. You've played with

her lots of times." I pried Hannah free and handed her over. She started to whimper, reaching back toward me. "I'm sure she'll be all right when you get her outside."

Sally took her and headed to the backyard. "We'll be fine."

I pulled the tomatoes and lettuce out of the fridge and put them on the cutting board. Then I stepped into the living room to look out the window at how Hannah was doing. Sally was offering Hannah a potato chip; Hannah turned away.

Babies are emotional barometers. They always know when I'm tense. Oh, well, she'll live through this. She's safe with Sally.

A few minutes later, I pushed through the back door with my plate of lettuce and tomatoes in hand. I glanced over at the charcoal. Good. It was ready for the hamburgers. Hannah wasn't crying. Great. I looked around to locate her.

Hannah was not safely wrapped in Cousin Sally's or Aunt Susan's arms. She was standing seven feet above the ground, perched atop Papa's big hands. His arms were fully extended, with his hands wrapped around Hannah's thighs while she balanced above his head like an acrobat. With her arms slightly raised to keep her equilibrium, Hannah teetered back and forth, a gleeful grin lighting up her rosy cheeks. I stood still, holding my breath, as if my slightest movement might upset her balance and send her tumbling to the ground.

Don had done this trick with all of our children. No one had ever fallen, but I had never gotten comfortable with his defying gravity with my babies. After what seemed hours, Don pulled Hannah down and cradled her in the crook of his arm. She laughed, enjoying the quick ride from her lookout station.

I put the tomato plate on the serving table then walked over to Don. A sudden urge to hold Hannah had come over me. "Some trick you've got there." Hannah smiled and kicked her feet, making no gesture for me to take her.

Don said, "Relax, honey. She's perfectly safe. She's with her Papa."

I couldn't figure out how Hannah could feel safe seven feet off the ground—when she didn't feel secure wrapped in a loving relative's arms. But this time I took my stress reading from Hannah. Her contented, shining eyes told me all I needed to know—she knew she was safe in her Papa's hands.

God is strong and able to sustain us. It helps us to realize God's promise to be our refuge if we meditate on God going with us and holding us up throughout the day. If we envision God going ahead of us into the places we will go, providing us with the strength, love, and wisdom we'll need, it can help us to face with peace and assurance the time, the tasks, and the people in our upcoming day. God is our ever-loving place of rest and safety.

$\mathcal{D}$ADDY'S PROMISE

JEFF ADAMS

"D addy, are you coming home?"

I'd been gone two days and I'd be home in three more. But at that moment, I wanted to say, "I'm on my way." I wanted to hang up the phone, leave the conference, and catch the next flight.

I wanted to give Meaghan what she needed. I longed to pick her up, twirl her around, smother her with hugs and kisses, and say, "I missed you and I love you." I wished I could wipe away her tears and rock her to sleep as I did the day she was born.

"Daddy, are you coming home?" She didn't ask when I'd be home. She asked if I was ever coming back. She wasn't just lonely; she felt abandoned. She thought I had deserted her. We adopted Meaghan at birth, and now she wondered if I'd always be her daddy. It didn't matter that I promised to return. The fact that her mother was with her gave her little comfort.

"I miss you, Daddy."

"I miss you too, honey. Can you let me talk to Mama?"

I told my wife, Rosemary, "Hold her close. Someone has to take my place while I'm gone."

I never want Meaghan to be sad or hurt. What kind of father would leave his child and let her suffer?

That's the question we're tempted to ask when we suffer. "God, where are you?"

Sometimes God seems more distant when we need him most. When the doctor says, "I'm sorry." When the policeman says, "There's been an accident." When the one who vowed they'd always be there says, "I'm leaving."

If God loves us, how can he allow bad things to happen to us? If he is all-powerful, if he knows what's going to happen, why doesn't he intervene?

The moment such questions come to our minds, we're tempted to question God's character. We feel abandoned. Deserted. Betrayed. We need to hear his voice.

Jesus understands our feelings. He felt the same way. He even asked his father the same question. "Why have you forsaken me?" (Matthew 27:46). In the midst of his suffering he didn't understand why his father didn't intervene, but he never doubted his father's promises.

When Meaghan and I spoke on the phone she could hear my voice, but she couldn't see me. Just as Meaghan couldn't see me, we can't see our Father. But, like Jesus, we can hear our Daddy's voice. And when we do, his words comfort us.

I assured her that I'd return soon. And before I hung up, she told me all the things she wanted to do when we were together again. She didn't understand why I was so far away, but she believed me when I said I'd come back.

Jesus promised that he'd come back. God promised that he'd never abandon us. And we can count on Daddy's promise.

$\mathcal{Y}$OUR RIGHT TO KNOW WHY GOD DOES WHAT HE DOES

BRUCE WILKINSON

from *Secrets of the Vine*

W e're born with the conviction that we deserve to be in control of our lives. Yet this assumption is in conflict with the
life of faith. That's why very early in mature pruning, God will ask
you to give up your "right" to know why certain things are happen-
ing to you.

When he was very young, I took our son David to the hospital
for a shot. As the doctor approached with needle in hand, David
bolted. When I finally corralled him behind a planter and swung
him up into my arms, I saw the terror in his face. How can you
explain to a sick toddler that his body needs penicillin? Yet David
stayed in my arms as the doctor prepared to give the injection. When

the moment came, David didn't push me away. Instead, he held on more tightly and cried out, "Daddy!"

We go through long seasons in our faith walk when we're unable to answer questions like Why? and How long? We only know Who—our loving Father—and He has proven worthy of our trust. He asks us to let go of reasons, of rights, of fears, and simply throw our arms around His neck. At those times we can pray: "Father, I'm hanging on to You. You can do whatever You want. Just carry me through."

THE EXAMPLE OF A FATHER

ERR OUT!

CLARK COTHERN

from *Night Light for Parents*

My father gave me a great example of character when I was a boy watching a church-league softball game. Dad was forty-three at the time and very active. Though he wasn't known for hitting grand slams, he was good at placing the ball and beating the throw. Singles and doubles were his specialty, and he did the best he could with what he had.

This particular dusty, hot Phoenix evening, Dad poked a good one right over the second baseman's head, and the center fielder flubbed the snag and let the ball bloop between his legs.

My dad saw this as he rounded first base, so he poured on the steam. He was five feet ten inches, 160 pounds, and very fast. He figured that if he sprinted for third and slid, he could beat the throw.

Everyone was cheering as he sent two of his teammates over home plate. The center fielder finally got his feet under him and his fingers around the ball as Dad headed toward third. The throw came as hard and fast as the outfielder could fire it, and Dad started a long slide on that sun-baked infield. Dust flew everywhere.

The ball slammed into the third baseman's glove but on the other side of Dad—the outfield side—away from a clear view by the ump, who was still at home plate. Our team's dugout was on the third base side of the diamond, and every one of the players had a clear view of the play.

Dad's foot slammed into third base a solid second before the ball arrived and before the third baseman tagged his leg. But much to the amazement—and then dismay—and then anger—of the team, the umpire, who hesitated slightly before making his call, yelled, "Yerr out!"

Instantly, every member of Dad's team poured onto the field and started shouting at once—Dad's teammates were intent on only one purpose: They wanted to win, and by golly, they knew they were right!

The two runners who had crossed home plate before Dad was called out had brought the score to within one. If Dad was out— and we all knew he wasn't—his team was potentially robbed of a run.

With only one inning left, this one bad call could cost them the game.

But just as the fracas threatened to boil over into a mini riot, Dad silenced the crowd. As the dust settled around him, he held up a hand. "Guys, stop!" he yelled. And then more gently, "There's more at stake here than being right. There's something more important here than winning a game. If the ump says I'm out, I'm out."

And with that, he dusted himself off, limped to the bench to get his glove (his leg was bruised from the slide), and walked back into left field all by himself, ready to begin the last inning. One by one, the guys on his team gave up the argument, picked up their own gloves, and walked out to their positions on the field.

I've got to tell you, I was both bewildered and proud that night.

My dad may have been dusty, but I saw a sparkling diamond out there standing under the lights, a diamond more valuable than all the runs his team might have scored.

For a few minutes that evening I was a rich kid, basking in my father's decision to be a man, to hold his tongue instead of wagging it, to settle the dust instead of settling a score. I knew what he showed me at that selfless moment was worth more than all the gold-toned plastic trophies you could buy.

Dad held court that night, and everyone on the field and in the crowd was a member of the jury. When the verdict came in, their decision was unanimous: This was a man of character.

WALKING IN MY DADDY'S SHOES

BILL DAVID WALKER

M any times as a little boy I remember stepping into my
daddy's shoes and trying to make those size twelves fit while
struggling to walk across the floor. Even now, at age forty-nine, the
familiar memory of the *slip-thud, slip-thud* of those old work shoes still
brings a smile. The feel of my little-boy feet trying to lift those heavy
shoes while attempting to walk like my dad still tugs at my heart-
strings today.

My father, William E. Walker, Jr., not only had large feet but
also a big heart full of compassion for others. This love for others
touched not just our family, but the lives of all those who lived in
our small community. Around our store, I proudly wore the nickname of *Little Bill*. To this day some of the older people of Tipton
still call me that.

In those days people came into our store countless times and left
with unpaid-for groceries. After they left, we hung their charge tickets on a rotating file behind the counter, hoping they'd pay them off
when they could. Too many times, though, they never paid, and the

tickets were moved from the rack to a box in a file drawer. Around our town, our store's nickname was "Walker Welfare" because Daddy was the only man in town who continued to offer credit to people who failed to pay their bills each month.

Daddy blindly trusted everyone. Instead of depositing his money bag in the bank's night deposit each evening, he took it home and hid it behind his bedroom door. At times that bag contained several thousand dollars. His reasoning was "You never know when an emergency might come up, and someone might need help."

Those emergencies came up often. Our doorbell rang at all hours of the night, because people knew they could rely on Daddy to help them when they needed it. He'd get the bag, unzip it right in front of them, and count out the money they needed. He'd tell them not to worry about signing anything; he'd make a ticket the next morning and hang it on the rotating file.

When we sold the store in 1978, I found him behind the building, burning a box full of charge tickets. I tried to rake some out of the fire. "Daddy, what are you doing? Don't you know you're burning money?"

He waved me away. "I've done this twice before. It's no big deal."

"How much have you burned?"

"Well," he shrugged, "this box alone amounts to almost $250,000."

"A quarter of a million dollars!" I couldn't believe it. "Think how we could live if we had that much money!"

"Do you really think a quarter of a million dollars would make us better people?"

Guiltily, I touched the unburned tickets. "Probably not, but . . ."

He put his arm around my shoulders. "Remember, son, some can't afford to pay, and that's all right. As for those who can—I know they owe it, they know, and God knows. I promise you this one thing: If it doesn't come out in the wash, I guarantee it'll come out in the final rinse."

When Daddy died in 1981, I inherited that old revolving ticket rack. While going through it a while back I found, in the drawer beneath it, some tickets that he'd missed. Teary-eyed, I tore them up and dropped them like confetti into our dumpster.

Watching them floating in the late afternoon sun, I think of the shoes I'm still trying to fill. I know I'll never be able to fill them completely, but I wouldn't trade one day of his walking beside me, holding my hand as I slip-thudded through the house in those over-sized shoes, for even one penny of that quarter of a million dollars and all the interest it would have earned over the past thirty years. My dream is that my own sons will want to walk in my shoes.

THE BEST GIFT EVER

JULIE GARMON

O n an early spring day, with trembling hands and a heart as bare as the dead of winter, I drove to Mulberry Grove, my grandparents' new assisted-living facility. I wanted to cheer up Daddy Robert and Westie, my father's parents, but nothing about that day felt hopeful.

After my father died twenty years ago, I knew the time would come for me to assume the care of my grandparents. I'd dreaded it for years, because I didn't know how to talk to Daddy Robert.

We were so different. He kept his affection for others tucked neatly away in his pocket like an ironed handkerchief.

An aching memory still jabbed at me. I was sixteen and had saved to buy him a birthday present—a bird feeder that looked like a country store, the perfect gift for my rural grandfather. He tore into the paper and said, "You should save your money. Birds can fend for themselves." Grimly he trudged outside to hang it. I stared up at the ceiling to contain my tears. *I can't make him smile. It's impossible.*

Now, almost thirty years later, I had admitted him, at the age of ninety-one, to the hospital for surgery. Then I made the two-hour drive to check on Westie and promptly called an ambulance for her. She'd become dehydrated and disoriented without my grandfather. Even harder than caring for them was trying to communicate with my aloof grandfather.

Only three things excited Daddy Robert—his vegetable garden, a freezer full of food, and saving money. Once I surprised him with a six-pack of cold Coke. He demanded I exchange it for a two-liter bottle. "Wasted money," he'd muttered.

I wanted to scream, "Don't you want to talk about things that matter, old man? You saved twelve cents. Who cares?" Earlier that year, he'd insisted I call the president of his hometown bank at night and ask for a better rate of return on his CDs.

One March morning I was bringing some papers for my grandfather to sign from his investment broker. I also had some daffodils I'd picked for Westie, but the vase tipped over in my Jeep and spilled water all over the document.

God, this is too hard. I can't do it. I don't care about interest rates and mutual funds.

Pushing open the thick glass doors at Mulberry Grove, I spotted my stepfather, Gene Acuff, a retired sociology professor and minister. He had married Mom four years after my father died. He visited old people *for fun*—even strangers. Thankfully, Wednesday was his regular day to hang out at Mulberry Grove.

Gene whistled and carried a newspaper under his arm. "Hey, there." He hugged me hard and studied my expression. "It's going to be okay. You'll see."

"I'm so glad you're here." I clutched his arm. "I found a real estate agent to list their house, but Daddy Robert doesn't want to sell. He says they're moving back home." I waved the soggy document in front of his face. "And look. I drenched his important paper work."

Gene kept smiling as though he didn't get it.

"What am I going to do? I can't even talk to him, much less please him."

Gene kept right on smiling. His reassuring dimples showed. Then he spoke to me gently, as though I were in kindergarten. "First, take these wet pages back out to your Jeep. They'll dry in the sun. Second, watch me. Today is lesson one," he said in his professorial tone. He touched my elbow and led the way to the parking lot, then back inside.

I lagged a step behind to observe.

Daddy Robert and Westie sat in wheelchairs, side by side.

"You two are looking mighty spiffy," Gene said.

I slipped past Gene into the bathroom for water to add to the flowers. I cleaned the nightstand and picked up used paper cups and tissues and threw them away. I adjusted the blinds and anxiously peeked into the bathroom at their supplies. Tums, hospital hand lotion, denture cream—stuff I'd never bought or used.

"Got today's newspaper?" Daddy Robert asked, his hands firmly gripping the sides of his wheelchair.

"Got it right here. What section you want to hear first?" Gene sat down in the green recliner brought from their home. I eased down onto the worn chenille bedspread.

"Read me the obits. Then the stock market."

Money and death. What about relationships?

After Gene finished reading in a booming voice, he folded the newspaper and said, "Daddy Robert, tell me about when you were courting Miss Ada."

"Shoot. Back in them days we could go to the picture show and get a Coke for a nickel. Ain't nothing like today. Plumb highway robbery."

"I knew I loved him when he threw a snowball at me," Westie piped in. "I was fifteen. Been together now for seventy-five years." She smiled with her brown, almond-shaped eyes first. Then she smiled with her mouth, and all the coyness of a schoolgirl shone through. Westie smoothed her white pageboy hair and patted his thin tan hand weathered with years of hard work.

"Lemme polish those shoes of yours, Robert," Gene said, and gathered the polishing supplies. He knelt down as though serving a king and slipped off the thirty-year-old, worn brown shoes. Daddy Robert prided himself in squeezing a lifetime of use out of almost everything. Gene bent over him for a long time, asking about their lives—the rhythm of the hard black brush swishing as he spoke. Pretty soon, those shoes shone chocolate brown again.

"Nearly good as new," Gene said. "I've always wanted to know something. What's the secret for growing those tomatoes of yours?"

I can't believe it. Gene's good with him.

"Always buy Better Boys. And don't waste your scraps from the supper table. Put 'em in the garden. Bury you a milk jug for watering near each plant." He indicated an imaginary level of the ground. "Poke holes in the jug and fill it up. Then you won't have to turn on the spigot but once 'ta week."

I remembered back to summers of visiting Westie and Daddy Robert. I'd stand on the old peeling black-and-white linoleum floor and watch Westie slice fat tomatoes and arrange them on her Blue Willow china platter. She'd fry chicken, cut corn off the cob from their garden, and make a chocolate cake from scratch. Later on, about the time the lightning bugs dotted the yard, we'd slice an icy watermelon on the cement table out back. *Why can't we go back to the simple life? I didn't ask for this job.*

Gene prayed with them before we left. We waved good-bye, and Gene and I walked out into the sunshine.

"You make it look easy," I said.

"You'll do fine. Ask God to help you." He winked at me. "Never forget, they're just people. Find out what matters to them." As I buckled my seat belt I glanced over at the papers. Gene was right about one thing. The document had dried in the sun.

A few months later Westie's health went downhill quickly, and she died. I couldn't imagine my grandfather's grief. He finally agreed to sell his home of fifty-three years; he'd outlived his only two children and now his wife. I tried to cheer him with a can of peanuts and a pack of Juicy Fruit gum—things I remembered he'd kept around the house. He plopped them on the bedside table and never mentioned my effort. *It's no use. Nothing makes him smile.*

That sweltering July day I was desperate—a panicky kind of desperate. Daddy Robert really needed my love, and I didn't know how to show it. How to communicate it. Just then, Gene's words returned to me. *Ask God to help you.*

"Okay God, I'll ask. I need you. Really bad. Please help me." Right in the middle of the kitchen floor I dropped to my knees. "Show me how to help him smile. This very day."

Around eleven o'clock that morning, I clomped down the front porch steps to go visit Daddy Robert. There, sitting by the rocking chair like an Easter basket, was a brown paper sack. Peeking inside, I knew my dear friend from down the street must have been thinking about me and stopped by. She loved to share fresh vegetables. Inside that sack sat seven tomatoes, still warm from her garden.

Find out what matters to him. The second thing Gene had advised.

Homegrown tomatoes topped his slim list of favorites. Excited, and balancing the sack in my lap, I drove to Mulberry Grove. Their mossy dirt aroma filled the Jeep. I pictured Daddy Robert adding fertilizer to the red Georgia clay, as he'd done for a lifetime. "Ain't nothing going to grow from bad soil," he'd say.

I tapped at the door of his room. He didn't hear me so I tiptoed in. Every other time I'd visited Gene had come along with me, but somehow I felt God walking right beside me that day.

"Lookey, lookey what I brought," I said loudly so he could hear and jiggled the sack.

"What's that?" He kept his eyes closed and rocked in his green chair.

"Homegrown tomatoes."

Daddy Robert stopped rocking and reached into the sack. He pulled out a plump one. I didn't worry about stopping him to wash it. He bit in and popped open his eyes.

"Now, that there's a fine tomato." Tears rolled down his face along with tomato juice. "Thank you, Julie-babe. You 'member back when I grew 'em every year?"

"Sure do. Last summer I helped you pick them." My throat felt tight and I grabbed a tissue.

And then I saw him smile.

It flitted about his mouth for only a second or two, but it was there—a smile as glorious as a sunset.

Daddy Robert stretched out his shaky but strong hand and pulled me down close to his wheelchair. We hugged for a long time as I stood bent over him, my face in his thick white hair. One by one, he slowly held all seven tomatoes in his palm, satisfied with their weight.

After all these years and when it counted most, Gene, my stepfather, showed me how to reach my father's father. He pointed me back to my heavenly Father, who is intimately acquainted with each of us. God knew the one perfect gift to make a difficult old man smile, and he made it so plain that July day. He even arranged for homegrown tomatoes to be delivered to my front porch.

All I had to do was ask for help.

$\mathscr{I}$T'S PART OF LIFE

---◆---

Y V O N N E   O R T E G A

$\mathbf{A}$s my flight to visit my parents took off, I gripped the armrests. Not because I was afraid of flying. But because I feared what I would find when I got home.

"Mom's become forgetful," Dad said during the previous week's call, "but otherwise she's doing all right."

He didn't say much more. I had no idea what he meant. But then, that was my father's way of protecting me so I wouldn't worry.

Perhaps I should have caught on. Every week when I called, she always asked me for my son's address and phone number.

When I arrived, Mom and Dad greeted me at the airport with hugs and kisses. They both looked healthy. Everything seemed normal. Then my mother asked me how school was. I hadn't taught in four years. I gently reminded her I was a counselor.

"But you're a guidance counselor in a school," she said.

"No, Mom, I'm a community counselor."

She frowned and continued, "But you used to be a guidance counselor."

"No, Mom, I've never been one." She had been at one time, but not I.

Dad asked about my flight and suggested we stop at the grocery store on the way home. He asked my mother what she needed. She assured him she didn't need anything.

The next day my dad took us to the grocery store again for items Mom hadn't remembered to buy the day before. He didn't complain. In fact, he seemed eager to help her. On my third day there, I overheard Mom tell one of my brothers that Dad never took her to the supermarket.

"Dad has taken us two days in a row," I said.

She stared at me with a look of uncertainty in her big brown eyes but made no comment.

In a conversation with my dad, I told him I suspected Mom had the beginnings of Alzheimer's disease. He said she had an appointment with a geriatric specialist the following month.

One afternoon I suggested that we visit my Aunt Bertha and Uncle Arthur, who live five minutes from my parents' home. When I pulled out of the driveway, Mom stared to the left and to the right. She wrinkled her forehead, sat quietly, and let me be both driver and navigator. Now I understood why Dad drove her everywhere she wanted to go. She had no idea where she was.

Dad had changed his schedule to take care of Mom. He enjoyed his work as an electrical contractor, and he was good at it. However, he only worked part-time now. The day of my reunion with a cousin, Dad got up early, worked a few hours, and came home at lunchtime to take Mom to the beauty shop. He said nothing about how he missed his work and friends. He never mentioned the sacrifices he made because of the reduction in income.

The next day Mom wanted to write me a check. She gazed at me, turned to her checkbook, looked my direction again, and asked,

"What name do you go by?" She scratched her head with her pen and seemed to focus on my answer.

"My name is Yvonne Ortega."

"Do you spell Yvonne with one *n* or two?" Mom asked.

Tears came to my eyes, and I turned away from her to hide them.

On one occasion, my parents and I ate lunch at the mall. Mom ordered sweet and sour pork, which surprised me. She had never ordered fried foods or pork. Within hours of returning home, she hung over the commode vomiting and asked for ginger ale. Dad drove to the store to buy her some.

The whole week was one episode after another of Mom's forgetfulness. Dad patiently helped find her glasses, her purse, her scarf, her coat, and anything else she had misplaced. In spite of the snow and ice on the roads, Dad took us out to eat when Mom complained of being too tired to cook. He listened attentively as she told the same stories over and over. When they walked outside the house, he opened and closed doors for Mom and held her by the arm.

As I watched Dad take care of Mom during the rest of my week with them, I realized how much I loved him. Dad was there. Solid, faithful, never complaining. He anticipated Mother's needs and centered his life around her.

The evening before I returned home, Dad talked to me about Mom's condition. "I told your brother to be patient with her. It's part of life, Yvonne."

In that moment, I began to comprehend the unconditional love of my heavenly Father. I caught a glimpse of what it means for him to accept me as I am. I knew he would take care of me and never leave me or forsake me.

I had taken my father for granted. He was stable. Always there for the whole family. But now I saw him differently. His compassion and tenderness made me think of my heavenly Father. Sometimes I am guilty of taking God for granted, but he remains the same. His love for me doesn't change.

My mother's Alzheimer's disease continues to progress, and my father has become even more protective and loving. That's how God works, I thought. The more we need him, the more closely he hovers.

THE SECRET INGREDIENT

D E B R A   A Y E R S   B R O W N

S anta's coming tonight!" Daddy rushed inside from the cold north Georgia night, closed the door with his shoulder, and dropped a bag of navel oranges, nuts, and stick candy beside me on the floor. A box of Moon Pies, my favorite treat, rested on top.

I sat cross-legged in front of the crackling fire and stared up at the tall, broad-shouldered man with thinning hair and an engaging smile. Even at eight years old, I realized that Daddy, a hardworking man of few words, was an unlikely Santa. I also knew from past Christmas Eves that we'd deliver toys, clothes, and candy to a neighbor who Daddy said needed our help.

"It's almost nine o'clock," he said as I grabbed the Moon Pies, anticipating the joy of biting into the chocolate covered cookie sandwich with the marshmallow filling. "The presents for the Reynolds family are bundled up in the back of the truck."

I followed him to the kitchen to find Mom.

"Just in time to add the secret ingredient," she said to me and slid the first of four cake layers on a plate, then stuck holes in the layer with the point of a knife.

As I had done for the previous two years, I spooned on a bit of juice from two oranges and watched it seep into the cake. "There's no cake as good as Sara's." I repeated what everyone at her office said about her baking. Mom smiled, and I ran my finger over the mixer beaters, scooping the sugary icing into my mouth. "Yum," I murmured.

Mom iced the cake, and I retrieved the bowl of freshly grated coconut.

"Okay, it's ready to go," Mom said after sprinkling on the last of the coconut.

"What?" My mouth flew open.

"We're giving it to the Reynolds family."

"Not *our* cake?"

"Giving to others is what Christmas is all about," Dad said.

"But Mom can't make another one before Christmas," I said. "Can't we slice it and save some for us?"

"No." Mom placed cellophane lightly over the cake.

"Let's go," Daddy said, buttoning his jacket. He pulled my new wool coat from the peg by the back door and handed it to me. Mom carried the cake. I grabbed my box of Moon Pies and stepped outside.

The winter wind stung my face. I tucked the box under my arm, buried my hands in my pockets, and dashed to Dad's old battered '56 Ford pickup, which in no way resembled Santa's sleigh.

I slid across the cold vinyl seat. Mom settled beside me.

"Why doesn't Santa deliver their gifts?" I asked.

Mom glanced at Daddy.

"The Reynolds children don't believe anymore," she said.

The old truck bounced over the bumpy roads. I stared at the

cake jostling on Mom's lap and hugged the Moon Pies to my chest. *Maybe if they believed, we'd be able to keep our cake,* I fumed to myself as we stopped in front of the small wooden house. A single bulb burned on the porch, leaving the rest of the house dark and remote. A dog barked in the distance. I shivered and hoped they weren't home.

Daddy hopped out, eased the door shut, and left us in the truck. His work boots crunched across the frozen ground to the porch. The truck's heater whirred, but my breath still froze in the night air like smoke from a cigarette.

Within seconds Daddy returned with Mr. and Mrs. Reynolds.

Mr. Reynolds, the tallest and skinniest man I had ever seen, opened the door and leaned inside the truck. "Hello, ma'am," he said to Mom.

The dim light threw shadows across his thin, drawn face. He pushed back a lock of black hair from his wrinkled forehead. Dark, bushy brows framed eyes that sunk into his head like a skeleton's. "How are you, little one?" He extended a hand across Mom to me.

"Fine," I said and shook his bony, calloused hand. I remembered Daddy saying that he was an excellent carpenter when he was able to work. Even in the shadows I could tell he was sick. One night I'd heard Daddy telling Mama, "He's a proud man. He refuses to go to the hospital because he doesn't have the money to pay for it."

Mr. Reynolds backed up two feet and stood by his wife, a woman half his height, who was dressed in a flowered cotton house-coat and a pink threadbare sweater.

Mom stepped out of the truck and handed the cake to Mrs. Reynolds. They huddled together talking.

I clutched my box of Moon Pies and peered out the window.

Mr. Reynolds met Daddy at the back of the truck, accepted the bags of gifts from him, and started toward the house. After a few steps he stopped and let the bags fall to the ground. He turned around and walked back to face my dad.

I watched, spellbound.

After a few moments of silence, he said, "These toys and that beautiful cake—" He choked back tears. "Now we won't have to disappoint the children. We'll have a special Christmas celebration like we used to have." He wiped at his eyes with both hands. "I don't know how to thank you." He threw his arms around my dad and hugged him.

Daddy patted his back. "It's what Christmas is all about," he said, clearing his throat.

Mr. Reynolds nodded and picked up the gifts. A tear rolled down Mrs. Reynolds' cheek as she joined him.

"Wait!" I jumped out of the truck. "Take these," I said. "Everyone loves Moon Pies." I handed the box of my favorite treat to Mrs. Reynolds.

Daddy put his hand on my shoulder and squeezed. I climbed into the truck. Mom slid in beside me and cupped my hands in hers. My heart pounded against my chest. But now I understood why Daddy wanted to help Santa even if no one knew but us.

Daddy's giving heart showed me that God would provide all we needed so that we would be able to share with others. From that moment I believed in using the power of love and concern to give hope to others. Like Daddy said, "It's what Christmas is all about."

THE *Embrace*
OF A FATHER

THE SYNTAX OF PRAYER

RICHARD J. FOSTER

from *Prayer: Finding the Heart's True Home*

One day a friend of mine was walking through a shopping mall with his two-year-old son. The child was in a particularly cantankerous mood, fussing and fuming. The frustrated father tried everything to quiet his son, but nothing seemed to help. The child simply would not obey. Then, under some special inspiration, the father scooped up his son and, holding him close to his chest, began singing an impromptu love song. None of the words rhymed. He sang off key. And yet, as best he could, this father began sharing his heart. "I love you," he sang. "I'm so glad you're my boy. You make me happy. I like the way you laugh." On they went from one store to the next. Quietly the father continued singing off key and making up words that did not rhyme. The child relaxed and became still, listening to this strange and wonderful song. Finally, they finished shopping and went to the car. As the father opened the door and prepared to buckle his son into the car seat, the child lifted his head and said simply, "Sing it to me again, Daddy! Sing it to me again!"

Prayer is a little like that. With simplicity of heart we allow ourselves to be gathered up into the arms of the Father and let him sing his love song over us.

DADDY'S HUG

EVA MARIE EVERSON

I'm trying to remember a time when my father didn't strap a holster to his belt before walking out the door for work, but I can't. Every morning before kissing my mother good-bye, he reached to the top of the refrigerator where his gun had been safely stored during the night. He'd unbuckle his belt, slip the leather out of a couple of the loops, slide the holster on, and re-buckle. And then out the door he'd go.

It never occurred to me the amount of danger he was in for wearing that gun. Daddy, a graduate of the FBI Academy, worked for the Georgia Bureau of Investigation as a Special Investigator. He drove a state-issued car with a radio that squelched the voices of dispatchers, sending out information about crimes and criminals. He chased down murderers and thieves, even if it meant going without food or sleep for days. He won shooting contests and was considered among the best interrogators the state of Georgia had ever employed.

But, to me, he was just Daddy, the most special man in my life.

We lived in a ranch-style house in the middle of a 1960s quintessential middle-class neighborhood. My bedroom was at the far end front corner, with large windows stretching across the house's face and side. With the drapes pulled open, I had a clear view of the road toward the entrance of the subdivision. In the afternoons—on those days when Daddy wasn't away on some special case—I watched intently for his return home. As soon as I saw the car round the corner I headed to the front of the house, arriving at the door between the kitchen and the family room about the same time Daddy did.

I flung myself into his arms, the roughness of the gun's grip scraping against the tender flesh under my arm. Not that I cared. It could have taken off an inch of skin and I wouldn't have cared. *Daddy was home.* As his arms came around me, his fingers curled, scratching up and down my back until my knees buckled and he had to squeeze even harder to keep me from falling.

I giggled, "Stooooop!" but I didn't mean it. It could continue forever; when Daddy hugged me, nothing in the world could possibly go wrong. Everything in life was as ideal as I wanted it to be.

As little girls do, I grew up, married, and moved out of state, seeing Daddy only a few times a year. Still, with each greeting, my arms found their way around his waist and his fingers still scratched up and down my back. There was no gun, however. Not anymore. Daddy had retired and the pistol he'd worn at his side for so many years had been locked away in a safer place than the top of a refrigerator.

Then one day a call came. The kind of call a daughter can never plan for. From the other end of the line Daddy said, "I've got multiple myeloma, baby."

My knees buckled; this time there was no one to catch me.

"Daddy, no."

As he always has, Daddy reassured me that everything would be all right. In a week or so—just before Christmas, he said—he'd have the port-a-catheter (a surgically inserted device for administering chemo and drawing blood) put in and then, after the holidays, chemo would begin. "I'm going to beat this thing," he said.

I went back home for Christmas. My parents, long ago divorced, had agreed to have dinner together as a family for the first time in close to twenty years. On Christmas Day I stood in what was still my mother's home and watched for Daddy's car to come down the street, just as I had many years earlier. When it finally rounded the corner, I ran through the house and out the side door, reaching him just as he stepped out of the dark blue Lincoln. This time, as my arms went around him, the hardness of the port pressed against my temple.

"Careful, baby," Daddy said, but he squeezed tight, reassuring me with his hug.

Please God, I prayed. *Don't let my Daddy die. Not yet. Not yet.*

Daddy lived. He survived chemo and stem-cell replacement therapy (where his own stem cells were used). It's been nearly four years since I felt the port against my head, half a lifetime since I felt the gun against my forearm. And though it appears we may be once again battling the "beast," I will forever know the peace of his arms around me.

When the time comes for me to let Daddy go to the arms of our heavenly Father, I'll draw comfort in what has always been there and is left behind. The sweet arms of the Holy Spirit, drawing me closer to the throne.

TO SUSIE WITH LOVE

E M I L Y   S U E   H A R V E Y

I adored my daddy. After he died in an automobile accident, I felt a huge part of me was missing. There was no way to bring him back, and after my tears subsided, depression set in. I realized that I needed to work through my grief in a positive way, and at the same time I wanted my grandchildren to know their papa. My stories of him entertained them, but I knew that wasn't enough.

I prayed, "Lord, please help me find a way through this."

As I finished my prayer, I knew what to do. *A memoir.* That way, I could work through my grief while sharing his legacy with the children. I wanted them to know that though he grew up in a share-cropper's family of fourteen kids, against all odds he survived and went on to rise above his humble beginnings.

I also wanted them to know the contradictions in Papa's character. Behind his gruffness and thick mustache was a big ol' teddy bear who loved and who yearned to be loved. The facts about him came easily. He was a World War II veteran who refused a medal for bravery. He finished high school and completed business college under the GI Bill. Although never attaining affluence, he was an excellent provider who exemplified character and integrity. Handsome. Noble. Musical.

Those were the facts. But that didn't provide a complete picture of Dad.

It wasn't enough. I worked at my computer most of the day, but nothing rang true. What stared back at me from the screen was lifeless and boring. I couldn't bring Daddy to life.

If only he were here to fill me in. If only I'd listened to him more.

That night in bed I prayed and asked Father God's forgiveness for all the times I'd not listened to his voice, just as I'd not always heard Daddy. *Thanks for caring,* I told him. *With Daddy gone now, I need your strength even more.*

When I rose the next morning, a mild lethargy weighted my limbs and dulled my brain. I went to my computer and began to write. Midmorning, I reread my text. What I had *still* did not capture Dad.

I closed my eyes and willed stronger memories to come. I drew a blank. With a heavy heart, I realized that I'd exhausted my Dad-data reservoir. I swiveled my chair away from the half-finished final sentence.

At lunchtime Lee, my husband, took one look at me and asked, "What's wrong?"

"There are so many gaps," I said. "Why didn't I listen more to his recollections of bygone days—poking fun at himself? And all those peculiar kinfolk." My shoulders slumped.

"You're missing him. That's the problem."

"Yeh. Funny . . . now I hunger for all those details of his. I grieve not only for him but for all the unfinished talks. I long to know all those he loved and who loved him."

Back at my desk, the bittersweet melancholy refused to lift. I said a prayer. From outside the window, a bird's song invaded my despondency.

"Music," I said, "That's what I need." I rummaged in my filing cabinet for some '50s music tapes to spring me from depression's snare. Nothing turned up.

Grief hovered. *Lord, please help me.* I returned to the filing cabinet and opened the same drawer I'd searched earlier. Where *are* those tapes?

In my search for the tapes I spotted a composition book jutting out from a folder. *Where did that come from?* I'd searched that area earlier and hadn't seen it. I started to push it back in line, and then I saw Daddy's handwriting on the cover.

Nothing about it drew recall—neither the tablet nor the filing. Then my vision honed in on Dad's scribbledy-script. Slowly, I reached to pull it out. His handwriting filled the entire back cover.

Across the front cover, in his familiar handwriting, were these words: "A History of James H. Miller and his ancestors. This is not a complete history, mind you, only recollections I've committed to memory. A faulty memory at that."

That last visit, a hectic time a few weeks before his death, he must have slipped it into the filing cabinet while I dashed about hosting dinner. I had been too busy, as usual, to notice.

"Thank you, Lord," I whispered again and again. I wiped away my tears and sat down to read. As I read, I began to understand my dad more fully. He not only mentioned events, but he shared his feelings and thoughts. Slowly, a three-dimensional James emerged. I met my great-great grandfather, a wealthy landowner who emigrated from England in the early 1800s and sired three sons. Tongue-in-cheek, Dad revealed how Bill (his dad, whom he compared to *Tobacco Road*'s Jeter) proceeded to waste every penny of his inheritance.

Colorful kin paraded by, fascinating and engaging me. There were the vignettes of each of us, Dad's children, that kept me laughing and weeping until, hours later, I read the last passage: "Ahhh, those precious kids of mine. I miss them sitting on my lap, now too old for Daddy to hug and kiss them. To me they'll always be my little ones. How I love them."

Tears of awe flowed as I thought how Daddy couldn't be with me but he left something special for me: his journal of love. He knew I would one day find it and *know*. And I thought how my heavenly Father, too, left me a book to read—his Word. Both my fathers wanted me to come to fully know and understand the depth of their love.

Father God knew the perfect timing.

My melancholy was gone. I'd spent the afternoon with my father. This time, Dad did all the talking. And my, oh my, did I listen.

When I got up to put away the notebook, I saw the last words, written on the front page of the composition book: *To Susie with love.*

The tears flowed a long time. Although I had known about my dad's love as I read the pages, the final words touched me deeply: *with love.* Dad's message was so like God's love book. Both are special, just as my earthly father and heavenly Father are to me.

THE HERO

B E T S E Y   G I B B S

as told to Kathy Winchell

A t seven A.M. I watched my father back out of our driveway to begin his twenty-four-hour shift at County Fire Station Number Four. I cried for him to stay. Despite my pride in his chosen profession, I worried for his safety and feared he might never return. I longed for the following morning when he'd come back to me; but when morning came, it brought the realization of my fears.

Fire fighting was more than a job to my father—it was a calling. He loved it so much; he strapped on his helmet and jeopardized his life for strangers. People called him a hero. To me, he was Dad. When he finished his shift, he would return home to lay down his life for another love—his family.

An hour after my dad left, I stepped onto the Snellville City Elementary School bus to begin my day. First school, then homework and dinner, followed by a couple of television shows before I climbed into bed next to my mom. I slept there each time my dad stayed at the firehouse. After tucking the blankets around me and kissing my forehead, she reached for the light. Suddenly she froze.

Then, like a deer alerted to human presence, she listened intently to the emergency signal sounding from my dad's police scanner. She sprang from the bed and turned up the volume.

Hand-held radios clicked and hissed across the channels; voices faded in and out as firemen relayed details of the blaze to one another. Amid the ping-ponging of information, we learned the county had dispatched my dad's station to a house fire. Three fire fighters had entered to rescue people thought trapped by the flames. When Dad's voice came over the airwaves from inside the house a shiver ran up my spine.

I always beamed proudly when I heard his voice resonate from the scanner like a well-known radio personality. This time, however, my stomach knotted. I squeezed my pillow and leaned toward the radio, willing him to escape unharmed. The continual sound of his voice kept me rooted at the edge of the bed. Then it was gone. I caught four words of the fire chief's next transmission. *Roof collapsed. Firemen trapped.*

We heard no further communication regarding my dad. Agonizing minutes turned into hours as Mom waited by the phone while I fought to keep my eyes open. After a valiant effort, I lost the struggle. I didn't hear my mom receive the predawn call.

When I woke in her king-sized bed, alone, alarm propelled me from the bed into the hallway at the top of the stairs. Below, my mom lay sprawled on the couch. I stumbled down the stairs.

"Where's Daddy?" I asked, barely able to get the words past my dry throat.

Mom's gaze drifted to the other side of the room. Mine followed. There, beside the fireplace, Daddy sat hunched in his favorite recliner. Bandages covered part of his face and neck, not entirely concealing raw skin from second- and third-degree burns.

Despite my relief, tears blurred my eyes. I'd never seen my dad badly injured. He had always returned from a shift ready to scoop me into his strong arms. I needed that now. I wanted him to hold me and tell me that everything would be okay. Instead, he groaned, his face contorting in pain. I stepped back.

He must have noticed my hesitation, and despite his discomfort, he smiled and reached for me. I ran into his open arms. He reeked of smoke, reminding me that he'd been in harm's way, but I snuggled closer, relishing the warmth of his embrace. He was safe—home—mine once again.

I have never forgotten that day. The fear. The sadness. The relief. But mostly what God showed me through my father's example.

My father loved fire fighting enough to risk his life for other people.

He loved *me* enough to fold me into weary arms and soothe my fears.

When anxious thoughts riddle my spirit, God reminds me of that day. He reminds me that he—the One who laid down his life for all people—reaches out to me with his wounded arms. And if I run to him, I'll find comfort in his loving embrace.

AN EARTHLY GLIMPSE OF HEAVENLY LOVE

VONDA SKINNER SKELTON

D addy was the first. The first one I loved unconditionally. The first one I loved unselfishly.

Other loves came and went. Some even came and stayed, like the precious love of my wonderful husband. But my love for Daddy was the first love that was totally pure—void of bias and ulterior motive.

Every encounter, every memory of my daddy was one of tenderness and gentility. Even as a child, I was enraptured by his words, captivated by his laugh, and thrilled by his presence. And although I gave him many opportunities to be angry, I never felt his anger. I felt his hurt instead. I could see the disappointment in his eyes ... and it broke my heart.

Daddy didn't have to use anger to rule me. Because of his pure, sweet love, he had my devotion; and devotion was a much greater incentive to obey.

I know my daddy made many mistakes, some of which were life-changing for those around him. But he succeeded in one area of his life that was most important to him. I never questioned his love.

It was only after his death that I realized the purity, the simplicity, the uniqueness of that love. No angles, no checks and balances, no give and take . . . just give. And that's what he did. He sacrificially gave his approval, his comfort, his encouragement, his love.

He's been gone twelve years, yet his wise words still speak to me every day. "Your husband is a rock, lean on him." "Your children are your legacy, build them." "Your grandmother was a saint, and you're just like her."

Daddy was wrong about one thing—I'm not a saint. But because of him, I *am* striving to reflect the love and gentleness of my heavenly Father, the One who loves me unconditionally, void of bias and ulterior motive. And even though he has a right to be angry with my sin and disobedience, he loves me with a pure and simple love. No angles, no checks and balances, no give and take . . . just give. And that's what he did—he gave his life for my sin.

I'll never be able to fully understand the depth of God's love for me, but I've had an earthly glimpse into the nature of my heavenly Father. I can believe he loves me beyond measure. I can believe he would take me in his arms and comfort me. I can believe he would die for me, because I know real daddies would die for their children.

My daddy wasn't perfect; I know that. But his unconditional love and sacrificial life pointed me to the One who was and is exactly that—perfect. Because of my earthly daddy, I will never question whether my heavenly Father loves me. I know his embrace and rejoice in his amazing love.

$\mathcal{P}$ERMISSIONS AND ACKNOWLEDGMENTS

Every effort was made to secure proper permission and acknowledgment for each story in this work. If an error has been made, please accept my apologies and contact Bethany House Publishers at 11400 Hampshire Ave. S., Minneapolis, MN 55438 so that corrections can be made in future editions.

Permission to reprint any of the stories from this work must be obtained from the original source. Acknowledgments are listed by story title in the order they appear in the book. Heartfelt thanks to all the authors and publishers who allowed their work to be included in this collection.

"Is There Something You Should Say to God?" by Bruce Wilkinson. Excerpted from *Secrets of the Vine* © 2001 by Ovation Foundation, Inc. Used by permission of Multnomah Publishers, Inc.

"Picture Perfect," by Jean Davis. Copyright © 2005. Used by permission. All rights reserved. Jean Davis's gratitude list includes hot and cold running water, her husband's sense of humor, and sunlight through her kitchen window. A contributor to *The Heart of a Mother*, *Whispering in God's Ear*, and *Cup of Comfort Devotional for Women*, her greatest writing challenge is composing the fifty-word bio.

"The Father as Savior," by Bryan Davis. Excerpted from *The Image of a Father*, by Bryan Davis. Copyright © 2004 by Bryan Davis. Used by permission of AMG Publishers. All rights reserved.

Lessons From a Father
"Just Wait Till January," by Kay Shostak. Copyright © 2005. Used by permission. All rights reserved. Kay Dew Shostak, like her daddy, is relying on God's wisdom as she and her husband, Mike, raise their three teenagers in Marietta, Georgia. Kay is President of the Atlanta Christian Writers' Group and a youth pastor at Wesley Chapel United Methodist Church.

"God's Creatures Great and Small," by Helen Kay Polaski. Copyright © 2005. Used by permission. All rights reserved. Helen Kay Polaski, series editor of *The Rocking Chair Reader* anthology books, has been a professional writer for thirty years. She was a newspaper reporter/ editor for seventeen years before becoming a book author/editor, poet, and screenwriter. Helen married her high school sweetheart, Thomas, and together they have three children.

Besides writing and speaking, her favorite activities are reading to and snuggling with grandchildren. Two of her books are *In the Pit: A Testimony of God's Faithfulness to a Bipolar Christian*, and *Guess Who's Special*.

Dr. Debra Peppers, a retired English teacher, was inducted into the prestigious National Teachers Hall of Fame. Now a university instructor, Emmy award-winning playwright, radio and television host, Debra is also a member of the National Speakers Association. Dr. Peppers is available for bookings at 314–842–7425 or drp@pepperseed.org.

A Father's Perspective
Bob Rose is first and foremost a husband to Kathy, father to three boys, and grandfather of six. He has led many lives, including car salesman, chef, musician, and teacher, but he found his niche as a Christian family counselor and pastor. He lives in Wyoming—the windiest and prettiest place on earth.

Diane H. Pitts writes about everyday occurrences that show God's love. She has plenty to write about with four men in her house. When Diane needs an escape, she works as a physical therapist at a Gulf Coast hospital.

Glenn A. Hascall is the author of three books and provides freelance work to several print and online publications. He is a child of God, the husband of one, and the father of two. These are counted among his greatest achievements in life.

Provisions of a Father
Susan Lare Baumgartel is a single mom, nana, businesswoman, and author. Her passions, beyond family, friends, and writing, are singing with Atlanta's Mount Paran Church of God choir, gardening, and decorating. Her forthcoming book, *When You're Fat, You Can't Polka,* reveals the lifelong challenges, strength, and heart of the obese.

Pamela Jenkins lives in rural Oklahoma with her husband and four children. She is the office manager of her husband's veterinary practice. Pamela supports 4-H and FFA youth activities and enjoys writing inspirational stories.

Bernita R. Caesar works as a registered nurse and director of education. She lives in Arvada, Colorado, with her husband, Sam, and a black lab named Jake. Their three children and five grandchildren reflect God's abundance and blessings. She uses her writing to inspire others to become aware of God's leading in their lives.

"The Check," by Kay Spivey Walsh. Copyright © 2005. Used by permission. All rights reserved. Kay Spivey Walsh grew up listening to her dad weave stories of their daily lives into lessons illustrating a relationship with the heavenly Father. Kay lives in the Shenandoah Valley of Virginia with her wonderful husband, two adorable children, a stubborn horse, and a loveable mutt. Kay teaches at James Madison University.

"Dad's Shoes," by C. Ellen Watts. Copyright © 2005. Used by permission. All rights reserved. C. Ellen Watts writes regularly for Christian and inspirational markets. Author of five books, with more in progress, this mom to five and grandmother to sixteen enjoys mentoring beginning writers, working in the church library, and speaking to young moms.

The Comfort of a Father
"Lost in a Crowd," by Judy Halone. Copyright © 2005. Used by permission. All rights reserved. Judy Halone is grateful for her parents' godly examples. She believes the ordinary moments from our childhood—funny or painful—can encourage others. Her column *Don't Make Me Turn This Car Around!* publishes weekly in Washington newspapers. She loves traveling with her family and watching her children grow.

"The Cake Bake," by Robert C. Peterson. Copyright © 2005. Used by permission. All rights reserved. Robert C. Peterson is still close friends with his father and considers him his prime example of Christian living. Robert is a Christian Church missionary, planting churches in Bogotá, Colombia, with his wife, Noelle, and kids, Niqelle and Russell.

Viejo, California, and writes about the transforming power of God. After serving twenty-four years as a communications professional in an international corporation, Sandra met God in a third-world village. Subsequently she began to write about God's faithfulness in the mission field of daily life.

"Nightmare in Second Grade," taken from *I Used to Have Answers, Now I Have Kids.* Copyright © 2000 by Phil Callaway. Published by Harvest House Publishers, Eugene, OR. Used by permission. All rights reserved.

Trusting a Father
"My Daddy Is Good," excerpted from *The Eyes of the Heart* by Tracie Peterson. Copyright © 2002 by Tracie Peterson. Used by permission of Bethany House Publishers, a division of Baker Publishing Group. All rights reserved.

"Just Wait," by Charles Harrel. Copyright © 2005. Used by permission. All rights reserved. Dr. Charles Harrel served as a pastor for thirty years before stepping down to pursue writing. He has over one hundred published works. His stories and devotionals have appeared in five books, including *Cup of Comfort Devotional* and *Christian Miracles.* Charles enjoys teaching, inspirational writing, and camping trips with his family.

"Trusting Papa," taken from *And Then God Gave Us Kids* © 2003 by Tamara Boggs. Published by Kregel Publications, Grand Rapids, MI. Used by permission of the publisher. All rights reserved.

"Daddy's Promise," by Jeff Adams. Copyright © 2005. Used by permission. All rights reserved. Jeff Adams is a freelance writer, teacher, and inspirational/motivational speaker. He lives in Arizona with his wife, Rosemary, and their daughter, Meaghan. Contact him at jeffadams@frontiernet.net or call 928–757–4580 to book speaking engagements.

"Your Right to Know Why God Does What He Does," by Bruce Wilkinson. Excerpted from *Secrets of the Vine* © 2001 by Ovation Foundation, Inc. Used by permission of Multnomah Publishers, Inc.

The Example of a Father
"YERR OUT!" by Clark Cothern. Excerpted from *At the Heart of Every Great Father* © 1998 by Clark Cothern. Used by permission of Multnomah Publishers, Inc.

"Walking in My Daddy's Shoes," by Bill David Walker. Copyright © 2005. Used by permission. All rights reserved. Bill David Walker has been married to his wife, Connie, for more than a quarter of a century. They have two sons, Leander and Davin. Bill is a school-teacher and a Church of Christ minister. He also works as a fund-raiser for Manuelito Navajo Children's Home in Gallup, New Mexico.

"The Best Gift Ever," by Julie Garmon. Copyright © 2005. Used by permission. All rights reserved. Julie West Garmon, like her mother, Marion Bond West Acuff, writes for *Guideposts*. Jerry, her father, died when she was twenty-three. She's incredibly grateful to her stepfather, Dr. Gene Acuff, whom she introduces as her dad. "He's the most merciful man I've ever met," Julie says. "He puts up with us."

"It's Part of Life," by Yvonne Ortega. Copyright © 2005. Used by permission. All rights reserved. Yvonne Ortega is the founder and president of the Peninsula Christian Writers. She has been published in *The Secret Place*, *The Quiet Hour*, *Believe*, and the Virginia Association of Alcoholism and Drug Abuse Counselors' *VAADAC Views*. She speaks at various events and teaches Bible classes and writing.

"The Secret Ingredient," by Debra Ayers Brown. Copyright © 2005. Used by permission. All rights reserved. Debra Ayers Brown, past president of Southeastern Writers Association, is published in *Guideposts*, *Woman's World*, *Chicken Soup*, the Chocolate series, *From Eulogy to Joy*, and more. Debbie, daughter Meredith, and husband, Allen, divide their time between Savannah and Hinesville, Georgia. Debbie's parents, Sara and Delmar Ayers, inspired her *giving spirit*.

The Embrace of a Father
"The Syntax of Prayer," excerpted from *Prayer: Finding the Heart's True Home* by Richard J. Foster. Copyright © 1992 by Richard J. Foster. Reprinted by permission of HarperCollins Publishers. All rights reserved. Additional permission granted by William Neill-Hall Ltd., Old Oak Cottage, Ropewalk, Mount Hawke, Cornwall TR4 8DW, United Kingdom 01209 891 427. Wneill-hall@msn.com.

"Daddy's Hug," by Eva Marie Everson. Copyright © 2005. Used by permission. All rights reserved. Eva Marie Everson is the author/coauthor of a number of works, including *The Potluck Club* (Baker) and *Sex, Lies, and the Media* (Cook). She is a nationally recognized, award-winning speaker and featured writer on a popular Christian Internet site.

"To Susie With Love," by Emily Sue Harvey. Copyright © 2005. Used by permission. All rights reserved. Emily Sue Harvey's stories appear in women's magazines, *Chocolate for Women*, *Chicken Soup*, *Whis-*

pering in God's Ear, and *From Eulogy to Joy.* Her two southern mainstream fiction novels, *Homefires* and *Unto These Hills,* are with the NY Peter Miller Agency. The novels appear under the pseudonym Suzanne Miller. Emilysue1@aol.com.

"The Hero," by Betsey Gibbs as told to Kathy Winchell. Copyright © 2005. Used by permission. All rights reserved. Kathy Winchell lives in Atlanta, Georgia, with her husband and two sons. Besides being an aspiring writer, she is a teacher and director for Atlanta Christian Youth Theater. She is also a member of American Christian Writers, Atlanta chapter.

"An Earthly Glimpse of Heavenly Love," by Vonda Skinner Skelton. Copyright © 2005. Used by permission. All rights reserved. Vonda Skinner Skelton is a freelance writer, speaker, and author of *The Bitsy Mysteries* for eight- to fourteen-year-olds. As an RN and health writer, her articles have appeared in many national magazines. She is a four-time winner of the Blue Ridge Christian Writers' Conference Scriptwriting Award.

More Stories
of Inspiration to Share With Those You Love

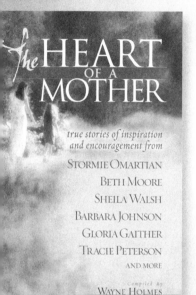

THE HEART OF A MOTHER

Enjoy real-life encouragement from Stormie Omartian, Max Lucado, Barbara Johnson, Tracie Peterson, and more. Written from the heart, each true story in this collection celebrates mothers and how much they mean to us. These moments of quiet will leave any reader feeling refreshed.

The Heart of a Mother
compiled by Wayne Holmes

THE HEART OF A TEACHER

For teachers in need of refreshment and all who owe a debt of gratitude to their teachers, this collection of inspiring stories brings long overdue honor to the unsung heroes who teach, coach, and mentor.

The Heart of a Teacher
compiled by Wayne Holmes